R. Vashon (Robert Vashon) Rogers

**The Law and Medical Men**

R. Vashon (Robert Vashon) Rogers
**The Law and Medical Men**
ISBN/EAN: 9783744667135
Printed in Europe, USA, Canada, Australia, Japan
Cover: Foto ©Suzi / pixelio.de

More available books at **www.hansebooks.com**

# THE LAW

## AND

# MEDICAL MEN

BY
R. VASHON ROGERS, Jr.,
*Of Osgoode Hall, Barrister-at-Law.*

TORONTO, CANADA,
AND
EDINBURGH, SCOTLAND:
CARSWELL & CO., LAW BOOK PUBLISHERS.
1884.

# PREFACE.

THE idea that in the library of nearly every practitioner in the professions of both Physic and Law there has been for some time a small gap among the books, which could be filled by a little work like this now submitted, has induced the author to prepare and publish the following pages.

While it is hoped that this little work will prove of use to the members of the Legal and Medical Professions, it is intended to be suggestive rather than exhaustive—a primer not an encyclopædia; and it is not expected that it will obviate the necessity for frequent conferences between physicians and lawyers whenever, in the practice of either, questions arise requiring the experience of the other.

In most cases the very words of the judges and reporters have been used, and if any expressions are noticed that may be deemed over strong it will be found that they are the words of others: the author's aim has been rather to act as an humble compiler and citer of cases, than to obtrude opinions or theories of his own.

Brief chapters on Dentists and Druggists have been given because of the intimate connection between these gentlemen and the members of the medical profession.

With great diffidence this book is committed to the tender mercies of the critics of these two learned professions—to those who can so effectually wield the pen, the tongue and the scalpel.

R. V. R., Jr.

Kingston, Ont., November, 1884.

# CONTENTS.

Preface .................................................... iii

Table of Cases Cited........................................ vii-xiii

## CHAPTER I.
Early Practioners and Laws.................................. 1-14

## CHAPTER II.
Fees........................................................ 15-31

## CHAPTER III.
Who Should Pay the Doctor................................... 32-41

## CHAPTER IV.
Who May Practise............................................ 42-54

## CHAPTER V.
Negligence and Malpractice.................................. 55-81

## CHAPTER VI.
Criminal Malpractice........................................ 82-92

## CHAPTER VII.
Professional Evidence....................................... 93-107

## CHAPTER VIII.
Medical Experts .......................................... 108-120

## CHAPTER IX.
Experts in Insanity Cases ................................ 121-128

## CHAPTER X.
Defamation ............................................... 129-137

## CHAPTER XI.
Relations with Patients .................................. 138-148

## CHAPTER XII.
Dissection and Resurrection .............................. 149-159

## CHAPTER XIII.
Dentists ................................................. 160-173

## CHAPTER XIV.
Druggists ................................................ 174-188

## CHAPTER XV.
Partners, Goodwill, Assistants ........................... 189-195

Index .................................................... 197-214

# TABLE OF CASES CITED.

## A.

Abernethy v. Hutchinson, 195
Adams v. Stevens, 17, 18
Adler v. Buckley, 20, 21
Ahearne v. Hogan, 141
Allen v. Davis, 140, 172
 " v. Eaton, 132
Allison v. Hayden, 16
Alpen v. Morton, 137
Anderson v. Burrows, 146
Andeureid's Appeal, 138
Anon, 134, 190
Anthony v. Smith, 106
Apothecaries Company v. Lotinga, 12, 16
Ashworth v. Kittridge, 102
Askin & Charteris, re, 27
Aswell v. Lomi, 142
Austen v. Boys, 191
Aveson v. Lord Kinnaird, 96
Ayre v. Craven, 132, 134, 135.

## B.

Bacon v. Charlton, 96
Baker v. London & S. W. Railway, 96
Ballon v. Prescott, 73
Barber v. Merriam, 96, 97, 117.
Barnes v. Means, 58
Barnstable v. Thatcher, 157
Basten v. Butler, 20
Bassett v. Spofford, 24
Battersby v. Lawrence, 16
Baxter v. Gray, 18, 19
Beekman v. Planter, 18
Bell v. Parke, 136
Bellinger v. Craigue, 21.
Bells v. Clifford, 28

Bergold v. Puckta, 131
Berier v. Galloway, 36
Bibber v. Simpson, 52
Billage v. Southbee, 140
Bill v. Neal, 130
Blackburn v. Great Western Railway, 81
Blake v. Midland Railway, 81.
Blackburn v. Mackey, 37, 39
Blogg v. Parkers, 20
Boardman v. Woodman, 113
Bogert v. Indianapolis, 153
Boone v. State, 188
Bowman v. Woods, 51, 53, 64, 100
Boyd v. Lappington, 33
Boynton v. Somersworth, 67, 148
Boyle v. Winslow, 166
Bracegirdle v. Orford, 157
Bradbury v. Bardin, 51, 120
Bradley v. Dodge, 33
Bradford v. People, 147
Brewer v. Dero, 157
Broad v. Pitt, 93
Brown v. N. Y. C., 97
 " v. Marshall, 179
 " v Sheppard, 99, 101
 " v. State, 143
Buchanan v. State, 29
Buell v. N. Y. C., 117
Burton v. Scott, 128

## C.

Cadwallader v. West, 139, 140
Cairo, etc., Railway v. Mahoney, 41
Caldwell v. Murphy, 97
Camp v. Martin, 133
Campan v. North, 94

Campbell v. Richards, 119
Carpenter v. Blake, 57, 58, 63, 64, 72, 73
Carnes v. Nesbitt, 193
Carson v. State, 148
Carter v. Baker, 114
" v. State, 103
Castner v. Sliker, 112
Cawdry v. Highley, 130
Chamberland v. Morgan, 70
Chapen v. Marlborough, 96, 97
Chicago, etc., Railway v. McKean, 68
Chicago, etc., Railway v. McGiven, 108
Chorley v. Bolcot, 16
Clark v. Gill, 26
Clarke v. Freeman, 132
" v. Hawke, 138, 139
Clark v. Kerwin, 69, 163
" v. State, 116, 124
Clay v. Roberts, 134
Cleveland, etc., Railway v. Ferry, 68
Cohen v. Continental Insurance Company, 95
Collier v. Simpson, 99, 103
Collins v. Grady, 19
" v. Carnegie, 134, 135
" v. Graves, 23
Colton v. Thomas, 172
Commonwealth v. Butterick, 187
" v. Cooley, 155
" v. Hackett, 91
" v. Hallett, 187
" v. Loring, 155
" v. Marshall, 155
" v. McPike, 91
" v. Ramsdell, 187
" v. Rich, 128
" v. Rodgers, 109, 124, 127
" v. Sturtevant, 100, 117
" v. Thompson, 84, 89
Connnecticut Mutual Life Ins. Co. v. Ellis, 100
Cooper v. Lloyd, 35
" v. Phillips, 38, 40
" v. N. Y. C., 41
Corsi v. Maretzek, 43, 51, 64, 115
Cossey v. L. B. and S. C., 96
Cox v. Midland Counties Ry., 41
Craig v. Chambers, 76

Craine v. Bandoine, 33
Crantz v. Gill, 37
Curtis v. Rochester, etc. Ry., 79

### D.

Davidson v. Nicholls, 183
Davis v. Mason, 193
" v. Ockham, 131
" v. State, 113, 117, 124, 126
Deane v. Annis, 38
Delafield v. Parish, 124
Demay v. Roberts, 145
Dement, Ex parte, 30
Denison v. Denison, 138
Dent v. Bennett, 139, 140, 172
Denton v. State, 97, 98
Dickenson v. Barber, 124
Dingnan v. Walker, 192
Dixon v. Smith, 134
Doggett v. Lane, 141
Duclos' Succession, 24
Duffit v. James, 21
Durnell v. Corfield, 142

### E.

Eakin v. Brown, 68, 163
Edington v. Ætna Life Ins. Co., 96
Edsall v. Russell, 131, 133
Ellis v. Kelly, 16
Emerson v. Lowell Gas L. Co., 112

### F.

Fairchild v. Bascomb, 112, 113, 125, 126
Farnsworth v. Garrard, 20
Farlar v. Lane, 141
Farr v. Pearce, 191
Fawcett v. Mothersell, 77
Fenwick v. Bell, 119
Fields v. Rutherford, 76
Fisk v. Wait, 69
Fletcher v. Fletcher, 146
Flint v. Bodenhamer, 124

Flower's Case, 130
Fox v. Glastonbury, 20
Forgery v. First Nat. Bank, 114
Foster v. Small, 134
Fraser v. Jennison, 94, 103, 106.

## G.

Gale v. Rector, 103
Gallagher v. Thompson, 20
Gardiner v. Heartt, 56
Gardner v. People, 117
Geiselman v. Scott, 68
Genshaw v. Germain, 17
Getchell v. Hill, 114
George v. Skivington, 183
Gibson v. Russell, 140
" v. Williams, 119
Gilman v. Andrews, 171
Gladwell v. Steggall, 75
Gramm v. Boener, 69
Goddart v. Haselfoot, 132
Granger Ins. Co. v. Brown, 159
Grattan v. Metropolitan L. I. Co., 95
Gray v. McLaughlin, 97
Greenough v. Gaskill, 93
Greonvelt's Case, 55
Greville v. Lylee, 142
Guthrie v. Weaver, 153

## H.

Haguenin v. Baseley, 138
Hains' Case, 152
Hall v. Semple, 146
Hammond v. Stewart, 26
Hancke v. Hooper, 58, 167, 194
Handey v. Heuson, 17
Haniline v. Commonwealth, 174
Hansford v. Payne, 182
Harbottle and Wilson re, 27
Harris v. Panama Railway Co., 103, 113
Harris v. Russell, 94
Harrison v. Bush, 136
" v. Grady, 33, 35, 36

Hartman v. Tegart, 36
Hartford Pro. Ins. Co. v. Harmer. 108
Harvey v. State, 104
Hastings v. Rider, 128
" v. Whitley, 193
Hathaway v. Nat. Life Ins. Co., 112
Haynard v. Young, 193
Hathorn v. Richmond, 61
Heald v. Wing, 113, 128
Heath v. Gibson, 59
Hegerick v. French, 80
Heinemann's Appeal, re, 48
Hewitt v. Prime, 95
" Wilcox, 18
Hibbard v. Thompson, 68, 69
Hides v. Hides, 140
Higham v. Ridgway, 106
Hill v. Featherstonhaugh, 21
Hills v. Home Insurance Co., 113
Hitchcock v. Burgett, 148.
Hoard v. Peck, 187
Hoener v. Koch, 118
Hoghton v. Hoghton, 138, 139
Hollenback v. Fleet, 177
Holmes v. Halde, 80
Hood v. Grimes, 65
Horner v. Graves, 193
Horton v. Green, 54, 112
Howe v. Young, 179
Hoyt v. Casey, 39
Hughes v. Hampton, 23
Huffman v. Click, 103
Humphreys v. Stilwell, 137
Hunn v. Hunn, 95
Hunter v. Blount, 64
" v. Ogden, 73
" v. Sharpe, 133
Hunt v. Lowell Gas Light Co., 126
Hupe v. Phelps, 21

## I.

Illinois Cen. Railway v. Sutton, 97
Indianapolis, etc., Railway v. Gaston, 79
Indian. and Cin. Railway v. Caldwell, 69

# TABLE OF CASES CITED.

## J.

Jackson v. Hyde, 77
Jarrett v. Jarrett, 124
Jauncey v. Knowles, 190
Jenkins v. French, 80
Johnson v. Robertson, 131
" v. Wills, 79
Jones v. Diver, 133
" v. Fay, 184
" v. Goodrich, 141
" v. George, 178
" v. Murray, 179
" v. Northmore, 78
" v. White, 108

## K.

Kannen v. McMullen, 21
Keily v. Colton, 164
Keith v. Lothrop, 116
Kennard v. Burton, 97
Kennedy v. People, 108, 119
Kerwhaker v. Cleveland, etc., Railway, 69
Kilborne v. Jennings, 114
Kingston's Case, Duchess of, 93
Kinney v. Nash, 135
Klock v. Burger, 174

## L.

Lamphier v. Philpot, 84
Landon v. Humphrey, 22
Langdon v. Mutual Life Insurance Co., 54
Lee v. Hamerton, 96
" v. Griffin, 169
Leighton v. Sargent, 58, 64, 67, 79, 118
Lett v. St. Lawrence & Ottawa Railway, 81
Lester v. Pittsford, 113
Linn v. Sigsbee, 120
Livingstone's Case, 113
Long v. Chubb, 132
" v. Morrison, 21, 57
Longmeid v. Holliday, 74
Lorg v. First German Cong. 113
Lovatt v. Tribe, 125
Luning v. State, 100, 105
Lush v. McDaniel, 97
Lynn's Case, 154, 158

## M

Mackenna v. Parkes, 190
Mahoney v. Nat. Widow's Life Ass. 96
Major v. Knight, 142
Mallan v. May, 193
Malton v. Nesbitt, 125
Marshall v. Brown, 101
" v. Peck, 179
Masons v. Fuller, 111
Matteson v. N. Y. C. Railway, 97, 117
Maxon v. Perrott, 170
May v. Thompson, 192
Meagher v. Driscoll, 157
Mendum v. Commonwealth, 113
Mertz v. Detweiler, 64, 118
Metropolitan Railway v. Jackson, 76
Michigan Cen. Railway v. Hasseneyer, 61
Middleton v. Sherbourne, 141, 143
Miller v. Beal, 23
Mills v. Perkins, 174
Mitchell v. Homfray, 141
" v. State, 119
" v. Connor, 147
Mock v. Kelly, 18, 25
Moises v. Thornton, 135
Morgan v. Hallen, 17
" v. Schuyler, 173
Morrison v. Harmer, 133
Morse v. Auburn, etc., Railway, 81
Morse v. State, 119
Murphy v. Kellett, 137

## Mc.

McAllister v. State, 124, 126
McCandless v. McWha, 58, 59, 61, 67
McClallen v. Adams, 26
McClurg's Appeal, 193
McEwan v. Bigelow, 114
" v. Milne, 138
McIntyre v. Belcher, 191
McLeod v. Wakley, 133
McPherson v. Chedell, 18

## N.

Newell v. Doty, 117
New England Glass Co. v. Lovell, 119
New Orleans, etc., Railway v. Allbritton, 111
Newton v. Ker, 23
Nickson v. Brohan, 194
Nicols v. Pitman, 195
Norton v. Sewall, 182

## O.

Ordway v. Haynes, 103

## P.

Page v. Barker, 118
" v. State, 126
Parker v. Adams, 68, 69, 163
Parkinson v. Atkinson, 26
Parnell v. Commonwealth, 114, 124
Patten v. Wiggin, 52, 57, 58, 62
Peacock v. Kesnot, 140
Pennell v. Cummings, 145
People v. Anderson, 103
" v. Hall, 99
" v. Monroe, 20
People v. Montgomery, 30
" v. McCann, 125
" v. N. Y. Hospital, 69
" v. Wheeler, 103
Perionowsky v. Freeman, 66, 70
Phillips v. S. W. Railway, 79
Pierson v. People, 95
Pinney v. Cohill, 101
Piper v. Manifee, 22, 167
Pippin v. Shepherd, 65, 74
Poe v. Mondford, 131
Polk v. State, 112
Popham v. Brooke, 140
Potter v. Warner, 63, 71
" v. Virgil, 36
Poucher v. Norman, 16
Pratt v. Barker, 140
Puryear v. Reese, 124

## Q.

Quafe v. C. & N. W. Railway, 98

## R.

Ramadge v. Ryan, 118, 119, 132
" v. Wakley, 132
Ray y. Burbank, 186
Reynolds v. Graves, 54
" v. Robinson, 120
Rhodes v. Bates, 138
Rice v. State, 84, 87, 89
Rich v. Pierpont, 59, 62, 117
Ripon v. Bittel, 100, 101
Ritchey v. West, 65
Roberts v. Johnson, 112
" v Kerfoot, 24
Robinson v. N. Y. C. Railway, 103
Rodgers v. Cline, 133
Roelker, *re*, 29
Rogers v. Cain, 97
" v. Turner, 38
Roosa v. Boston Loan Co., 98
Rose v. College of Physicians, 12
Rowell v. Lowell, 98
Ruddock v. Lowe, 65

Russell v. State, 128
Rutherford v. Evans, 135
" v. Norris, 110
R. v. Bennett, 194
" v. Burnett, 147
" v. Campbell, 46
" v. Case, 144
" v. Chamberlaine, 85
" v. Coll. Phy. & Sur., 45, 47
" v. " " " Ont., 148
" v. Coney, 144
" v. Crouch, 103
" v. Cuddy, 144
" v. Downes, 39
" v. Frances, 144
" v. Fraser, 147
" v. Gibbons, 93
" v. Gilles, 154
" v. Hannah, 147
" v. Hessel, 46
" v. Higginson, 125
" v. Hines, 39
" v. Lee, 91
" v. Long, 83, 86, 87
" v. Lynn, 154, 159
" v. Macleod, 66
" v. Markuss, 88
" v. Morby, 39
" v. Noakes, 56, 183
" v. Offord, 124
" v. Price, 154
" v. Richards, 125
" v. Rosinski, 144
" v. Searle, 120, 124, 125
" v. Sharpe, 153, 154
" v. Stanton, 144
" v. Simpson, 65, 84, 87.
" v. Smith, 40
" v. Spiller, 84
" v. Spilling, 85
" v. Stitt, 117
" v. Sutton, 147
" v. Tefft, 46, 190
" v. Tessymond, 194
" v. Thomas, 99
" v. Trick, 83
" v. Van Butchell, 84
" v. Vantandillo, 147
" v. Wagstaffe, 39
" v. Webb, 84, 90
" v. West, 147
" v. Whitehead, 117
" v. Williamson, 85
" v. Wright, 125

S.

Sainter v. Ferguson, 193
Scott v. Wakem, 146
Seare v. Prentice, 21, 64
Seavey v. Preble, 143
Secord v. Harris, 131
Sellen v. Norman, 40
Shafer v. Dean's ad'mor, 120
Shearwood v. Hay, 44
Sheldon v. Johnston, 24
Shields v. Blackburne, 65, 66
Simmons v. Means, 18
Simonds v. Henry, 58, 162, 168
Simpson v. Dismore, 18
Sinclair v. Rourk, 113
Sizer v. Burt, 106
Skinner v. G. N. Ry., 96
Skirving v. Ross, 134
Slater v. Baker, 59, 71, 168
Small v. Howard, 61
Smith v. Lane, 51
" v. Hyde 25
" v. Watson, 18, 34
Southey v Denny, 130, 132
Spaun v. Mercer, 33
Stackman v. Vivian, 38
Staunton v. Parker, 94
State v. Bowman, 117
" v. Clark, 118
" v. Cook, 112
" v. Dickinson, 147
" v. Fitzgerald, 147
" v. Gedicke, 147
" v. Hardister, 88
" v. Henkle, 112
" v. Hoyt, 104, 105
" v. Holmes, 174
" v. Knowles, 188
" v. Laffer, 187
" v. Jones, 117
" v. Powell, 117
" v. Reddick, 112
" v. Shultz, 85, 89
" v. Slagh, 117
" v. Slagle, 147
" v. Smith, 116, 117
" v. Sturtevant, 117
" v. Watson, 110
" v. West, 104
" v. Windsor, 126
" v. Wood, 111, 117
" v. Wray, 188

Stephenson v. N. Y. and H. R. Ry., 41
Stirling v. Thorp, 100
Street v. Blackburn, 166
St. Louis Mut. Ins. Co. v. Graves, 115
Suegoe's Case, 133
Summer v. State, 31
Sutton v. Tracy, 48, 54
Swain v. Tyler, 38

### T.

Tate v. State, 155, 156
Tatum v. Mohr, 114
Tingley v. Congill, 125
Thistleton v. Frewer, 52
Thomas v. Winchester, 180
Thorpe v. Shapleigh, 36
Todd v. Myers, 23
Toomes, re, 111, 113
Towne v. Gresley, 17
Tracy Peerage, 110
Tullis v. Kidd, 113
Tulty v. Alewin, 131
Turner v. Reynall, 44, 190
" v. Turner, 26
Tuson v. Batting, 19, 23
Twombly v. Leach, 117

### U.

U. S. v. McGlue, 126, 127
Utley v. Burns, 58

### V.

Van Bracken v. Fondar, 179
Van Tassel v. Capson, 135
Veitch v. Russell, 16
Villalobas v. Mooney, 23

### W.

Wade v. DeWitt, 104, 105
Wagstaffe v. Sharpe, 44
Walker v. G. W. Railway, 41
Wakley v. Healey, 135
Washburn v. Cuddihy, 103
Watling v. Walters, 33
Watson v. Vanderlash, 131
Webb v. Paige, 26, 28
Webber v. Shampake, 36
Wennall v. Adney, 40
Whetherbee v. Whetherbee, 128
Whalen v. St. Louis, etc., Railway, 79
Wharton v. Brook, 130
Wheeler v. Sims, 23
Whitcomb v. Reid, 171
Whittaker v. Parker, 110
White v. Bailey, 124, 125
" v. Carroll, 132
Williams v. Poppleton, 118
" v. Williams, 153
Wilmot v. Howard, 57, 70
" v. Shaw, 47
Wilson v. Brett, 65, 166
" v. Granby, 97
" v. People, 117
" v. Rastall, 93
Winans v. N. Y. & E. Railway, 113, 121
Wise v. Wilson, 194
Witt v. Witt, 97
Wohlfarht v. Beckert, 185
Woods v. Kelly, 37
Woods v. State, 188
Wright v. Proud, 140
Wynkoop v. Wynkoop, 153

### Y.

Yertore v. Wiswall, 80
Yoe v. State, 105
Young v. Makepeace, 116

# CORRIGENDA.

Page 5, line 23, *for* ousted *read* ousting.
" 8, line 3, *for* was *read* were.
" 12, line 17, *for* his *read* its.
" 24, line 19, *for* friend *read* friends.
" 43, line 18, *read* Hahnemann *for* Hahnneman.
" 55, line 6, *for* misdemeanour *read* misdemeanor.
" 85, last line but one, transpose the , and the ;.
" 96, line 7, *read* witnesses, can be excluded the
" 103, line 15, *for* Brown's *read* Browne's.
" 105, line 10. *for* words *read* works.
" 115, line 5, *for* opinion *read* opinions.
" 119, last line but one, *read* opinion of another etc.
" 138, line 1, *read* occupies *for* occupying.
" 173, line 12, *read* within.
" 175, line 4, *read* chemical.
" 177, last line, *read* venditor.

# THE LAW AND MEDICAL MEN.

## CHAPTER I.

### EARLY PRACTITIONERS AND LAWS.

THE first medical practitioners in England, of whom we have any record, were the Druids: these philosophers, theologians and soothsayers, also practised medicine and surgery, and were skilled in anatomy and physic. To add to the veneration in which they were held, to impress the ignorant masses with the idea that they had power with the gods and could prevail, and perhaps to cultivate a belief in the efficacy of the remedies provided, they mingled incantations and charms with their medicaments and nostrums. Their panacea was the mistletoe, cut from the sacred oak, with a consecrated hook of gold held in holy hands, on a mysterious night when the propitious beams of the waxing moon fell upon it; wrapped for a while in a sanctified cloth and treasured up in the holy of holies of the woodland god, this strange parasitic growth was deemed possessed of many virtues and was named All-heal. Two other herbs, the selago and samolus were also in those days highly valued for their medicinal efficacy.

To every healing herb a divinity was assigned by the Druids, and the good gods were ever ready to help suffering humanity against the evil genii who presided over the poisonous and unwholesome.

These priests also considered the creeping through *tolmens* (or perforated stones) good for many diseases. Their best charm, however, was the anguineum, or snake's egg, produced ('tis said) from the saliva and frothy sweat of a cluster of snakes writhing in a tangled mass, tossed in the air by the fierce hissings of the serpents, and caught ere it fell to the ground in a clean white cloth. A genuine egg, though encased in gold, would float against a running stream and do many another marvel. The Druid seems to have been a herbalist, a believer in the faith or prayer cure, as well as a homœopathist, for in taking the diseased plant, the mistletoe, to cure diseases he anticipated the doctrine of *similia similibus curantur*.

Even in those old days, according to Tacitus, there were female physicians who competed with the practitioners of the other sex. The wives of the Druids exercised the calling of sorceresses, causing considerable evil by their witchcrafts, but caring for warriors wounded in battle. Later on women seem to have enjoyed a pre-eminence as physicians and surgeons in England. Thus are we told that a "Mayd" treated a wounded "Squyre,"

> Meekely shee bowed downe, to weete if life
> Yett in his frosen members did remaine;
> And, feeling by his pulses beating rife
> That the weake sowle her seat did yett retaine,
> Shee cast to comfort him with busy paine.
> \* \* \* \* \*
> Into the woods thenceforth in haste shee went,
> To seeke for herbes that mote him remedy;
> For she of herbes had great intendiment.
> \* \* \* \* \*
> There, whether yt divine tobacco were,
> Or panachæa, or polygony,
> Shee fownd, and brought it to her patient deare,
> Who al this while lay bleding out his hart blood neare.

> The soveraine weede betwixt two marbles plaine
> Shee pownded small, and did in peeces bruze;
> And then atweene her lilly handes twaine
> Into his wound the juice thereof did scruze;
> And round about, as she could well it uze,
> The flesh therewith she suppled, and did steepe
> T'abate all spasme and soke the swelling bruze;
> And, after having searcht the intuse deepe,
> She with her scarf did bind the wound from cold to keep (a).

Of fair Nicolette we read—
> Her strength alone
> Thrust deftly back the dislocated bone;
> Then culling various herbs of virtue tried,
> While her white smock the needful bands supplied,
> With many a coil the limb she swathed around,
> And nature's strength returned.

Chirurgery, or surgery—that is manual application—appears to have been the earliest branch of the healing art. We are told of a wonderful cure effected upon Queen Elgiva, whose beauteous face had been mutilated by the brutal clergy. Many superstitious practices were in the early days mingled with the operations of the surgeons, as well as of the physicians. History speaks of a man the muscles of whose legs were drawn up and contracted so as to defy all the skill of the surgeons, until an angel advised wheat flour to be boiled in milk, and the limb to be poulticed with it while warm; then all was well.

From the tenth to the twelfth century the practice of medicine and surgery, in England, was almost exclusively in the hands of the monks and clergy. So lucrative did they find it that many of the monks devoted themselves entirely to it, to the utter neglect of their religious duties. This the authorities of the church disapproved of, and made many attempts to restrain. At last, in 1163, it was enacted by the Council of Tours that no clergyman or monk should undertake any bloody operation. From that time

---

(a) The Faërie Queene, b. III., cap. 5, sts. 31, 32, 33.

the clerics confined themselves to prescribing medicines, and the practice of surgery naturally fell into the hands of the barbers and smiths, who had previously been employed as assistants and dressers to the ecclesiastical operators.

The smiths soon found that most of the business was absorbed by the barbers: the latter kept little shops for cutting hair, shaving, bathing and curing the wounded, especially about the royal palaces and the houses of the great: the shops were marked by a striped pole and a basin, symbols that all the king's subjects might know where to apply in time of need; (the fillet around the pole indicating the ribbon for bandaging the arm in bleeding, and the basin the vessel to receive the blood). The barbers became so important that in 1461 the freemen of "The Mystery of Barbers, using the mystery or faculty of Surgery," obtained a charter from Edward IV., and were incorporated under the name of "The Company of Barbers in London," and none were allowed to practise save those admitted by the company. Although this charter was several times confirmed by subsequent kings, yet side by side with the regular barber-surgeons there grew up a body of men who practised pure surgery, and who actually formed a company, called "The Surgeons of London." In 1540, by Act of Parliament, these rival companies were united and named "The Masters, or Governors, of the Mystery and Commonalty of the Barbers and Surgeons of London."

The third section of this Act, after reciting that persons using the mystery of surgery oftentimes meddled and took into their cure and houses people infected with pestilence, great pox, and other contagious infirmities, and also used or exercised barbery, as washing, or shaving, or other feats thereto belonging, "which was very perilous for infecting the King's liege people resorting to their shops and houses and there being washed and shaven," enacted "that no manner of person within the City of London, suburbs of the same and one mile compass of said City of London, after the feast of the Nativity of Our Lord God then next coming, using barbery or shaving, or that hereafter shall use barbery or shaving within the said city, etc., he nor they, nor none of them, to his, her, or their use, shall occupy any surgery, letting of blood, or any other thing belonging to surgery, drawing of teeth only excepted; and furthermore, in like manner, whosoever that useth the mystery or craft of surgery within the circuit aforesaid, as long as he shall fortune to use the said mystery or craft of surgery, shall in nowise occupy nor exercise the feat or craft of barbery or shaving, neither by himself, nor by one other for him, to his or their use; and moreover, that all manner of persons using surgery for the time being, as well freemen as foreigners, aliens and strangers within the circuit aforesaid, before the feast of St. Michael the Archangel, next coming, shall have an open sign on the street side where they shall fortune to dwell, that all the King's liege people there passing by may know at all times whither to resort for remedies in time of necessity (a)."

In 1745 this union of barbers and surgeons was dissolved; or, apparently, the surgeons ousted the barbers, received a new name and all the privileges of the old company, with the exclusive right to practise within London and for seven miles around. In 1800 the Surgeons' Company was called "The Royal College of Surgeons, in London;" and this, in 1843, was changed to that of "The Royal College of Surgeons of England."

In Scotland, at a very early day, the chirurgeons and barbers were united, and enjoyed many rights and privileges. In 1505 the "craftes of Surregeury and Barbouris" were

(a) 32 Henry VIII., cap. 42.

formed into a college or corporation, by the town council of Edinburgh, and became one of the fourteen incorporated trades of the city. George the Third erected this corporation into a Royal College, and now it is known as "The Royal College of Surgeons of Edinburgh." In 1599, James VI., "to avoid the inconvenience caused by ignorant, unskilled, and unlearned persons, who, under the colour of chirurgeons, are in the habit of abusing the people to their pleasure, and of destroying thereby infinite numbers of his Majesty's subjects," incorporated the faculty of Physicians and Surgeons of Glasgow; and gave them jurisdiction over the City of Glasgow and the adjoining counties. A recent Act of Parliament has very much shorn the privileges of this faculty (b).

In Ireland, the "Fraternity of Barbers and Chirurgeons of the Guild of S. Mary Magdalene" was incorporated by Henry II. The apothecaries belonged to this body until 1745, when, with the aid of a statute, they set up for themselves, as "The Guild of S. Luke," or "The worshipful Company of Apothecaries." In 1784 the regularly educated surgeons of Dublin became incorporated under the name of "The Royal College of Surgeons in Ireland."

In the twelfth century medicine seems to have been first studied as a science in England. The Universities enacted that none should practise physic without passing through a certain course of study. In the fourteenth century the degree of Doctor of Physic was by no means uncommon. For many years physicians were greatly aided in chemistry and medical science by the discoveries of alchemists, and the search after the philosopher's stone and the elixir of life gave many useful hints to practitioners. Chaucer well describes a "Doctour of Phisike," in the Prologue to the

---

(b) 21 & 22 Vic. cap. 90.

Canterbury Tales, and gives an insight into the state of medical knowledge in the fourteenth century.

> ——— He was grounded in astronomie.
> He kept his patient a ful gret del
> In houres by his magike naturel.
>
> He knew the cause of every maladie,
> Were it of cold, or hote, or moist, or drie,
> And when engendred, and of what humour.
> He was a veray parfite practisour.
> The cause yknowe, and of his harm the rote,
> Anon he gave to the sike man his bote.
> Ful redy hadde he his apothecaries
> To send him dragges, and his lettuaries,
> For eche of hem made other for to winne:
> His frendship n' as not newe to beginne.
> Wel knew he the old Esculapius,
> And Dioscorides, and eke Rufus;
> Old Hippocras, Hali, and Gallien;
> Serapion, Rasis and Avicen;
> Averrois, Damascene and Constantin,
> Bernard, and Gatisden and Gilbertin.
> Of his diete mesurable was he,
> For it was of no superfluitee,
> But of gret nourishing and digestible.
> His studie was but litel on the Bible.

In 1421, under Henry V., an Act was prepared, providing that "no one shall use the mysterie of fysyk, unless he hath studied it at some university, and is at least a bachelor in that science. And saying, the sheriff shall inquire whether any one practises in his county contrary to this regulation; and if any one so practise fysyk he shall forfeit £40 and be imprisoned: and any woman who shall practise fysyk shall incur the same penalty." But this appears never to have become law.

It was not, however, until the beginning of the sixteenth century that modern British medical practice may be said to have commenced. And in 1511 was passed the first statute for regulating the medical profession (c). From the preamble of this Act we learn that physic and surgery was then practised by "ignorant persons, who could tell no letters on the book, and by common artificers, smiths, weavers, and women, who took upon themselves great cures, partly using sorcery and witchcraft, partly applying very noxious medicines to the disease."

Many years after this, however, were to be found those who though not "ignorant persons" approved of what would now be called sorcery, witchcraft and noxious medicines. Bacon gives the following as infallible cures for the whooping-cough: let a pie-bald horse breathe on the patient: give him fried mice, three a day for three days in succession: pass the sick person nine times under the belly and over the back of a donkey: feed the patient on currant cake made by a woman who did not change her name when she was married: or, hold a toad in the mouth that it may catch the disease. Burton, the Anatomist, says that an amulet consisting of a spider in a nut-shell, lapped with silk, is a cure for ague. Graham, in his "Domestic Medicine," prescribes spider's webs for ague and intermittent fevers.

By the statute of Henry the profession was for the first time divided into physicians, surgeons and apothecaries: a division still kept up in England. It also enacts, under a penalty, that "no physician or surgeon shall practise in London, or within seven miles of it, without examination by the Bishop of London, or the Dean of St. Paul's, and four doctors of physic; nor out of the city, or precinct, but if he be first examined and approved by the bishop of the diocese, or his vicar-general, calling to them such expert persons in the same faculty as their discretion shall think convenient." Fancy a D.D. sitting in judgment on an

(c) 3 Henry VIII. cap. 11.

M.D. How orthodox and regular in his attendance at church would the latter have to be! However, 14 & 15 Henry VIII. cap. 5, vests this power of examination in the President and Elects of the College of Physicians of London. This Royal College was founded in 1518 by letters patent from the king. Power was given to it to make laws for the government of all men of the faculty of physic in London and within seven miles, and for the correction of the physicians within those limits and their medicines: and none could practise within those limits without a license. Shortly after an Act of Parliament confirmed this patent so that none could practise in England without the license of the college, save graduates of Oxford and Cambridge. Subsequently Fellows of the college were given power, together with the warden of the Apothecaries' Society, to enter the houses of apothecaries in London, to examine their wares, drugs and stuffs, and to burn and destroy those that were defective.

In 1560, by 32 Henry VIII. cap. 40, surgery was declared a part of physic, and the practice thereof was thrown open to all of the company or fellowship of physicians throughout the realm. Not long afterwards the Parliament of this reforming king seems to have changed its mind and made a move in the direction of free-trade in physic, and by 34 & 35 Henry VIII. cap. 8, any man or woman was permitted to practise to a limited extent. We fancy we can trace the influence of the sturdy king in the provisions of this Act, which was entitled, "An Act that persons being no common surgeons may administer outward medicines notwithstanding the statute;" the statute after referring to the Act passed in the third year of the king's reign (which imposed penalties upon those who should practise as physicians or surgeons without being examined and admitted) goes on to say, "Sithence the making of which said Act (that of 3 Henry VIII.) the company and fellowships of surgeons of London, minding only their own lucres, and nothing the profit or ease of the diseased or patient, have sued, troubled and vexed divers honest persons, as well men as women, whom God hath endued with the knowledge of the nature, kind and operation of certain herbs, roots and waters, and the using and ministering of them to such as be pained with customable diseases, as women's breasts being sore, a pin and the web in the eye, uncomes of hands, burnings, scaldings, sore mouths, the stone, strangury, saucelin, and morphers, and such other like diseases; and yet the said persons have not taken anything for their pains or cunning, but have ministered the same to poor people only, for neighbourhood and God's sake, and of pity and charity. And it is now well-known that the surgeons admitted will do no cure to any person, but where they shall know to be rewarded with a greater sum or reward than the cure extendeth unto: for in case they would minister their cunning unto sore people unrewarded there should not so many rot and perish to death, for lack of help of surgery, as daily do; but the greatest part of surgeons admitted have been much more to be blamed than those persons that they trouble." It further states that "although the most part of the persons of the said craft of surgery have small cunning, yet they will take great sums of money and do little therefor, and by reason thereof they do oftentimes impair and hurt their patients rather than do them good." In consideration whereof and for the ease and health of the king's poor subjects, it was enacted that it should be lawful to every person having knowledge and experience of the nature of herbs, etc., to practise and minister them without suit or vexation. (Here is evidence of the existence of herb doctors, hydropaths and lady physicians in those days.)

Numerous Acts of Parliament have been passed touching the medical profession since the days of "Bluff King Hal," one under James I. to prevent popish recusants practising physic, or using or exercising the trade or art of an apothecary; another under William and Mary for exempting apothecaries from serving as constables or scavengers; another for exempting spirits and spirituous liquours used by physicians, &c., in the preparation of medicine from duty, and others for purposes too numerous to mention. But it is the Medical Act of 1858, as amended by 22 Vict. cap. 21, that now governs the practitioners.

In 1681, the Royal College of Physicians of Edinburgh, was incorporated and power was given of licensing practitioners and of preventing others practising. In Ireland, although the idea had been conceived many years before, it was not until 1654 that a body called "The President and Fraternity of Physicians" was founded; subsequently this company was incorporated and powers given to it very similar to those enjoyed by the London College. Under the Medical Act, Her Majesty was empowered to change the name of this institution (which had already enjoyed several aliases), to that of "The Royal College of Physicians of Ireland."

In England and Ireland a third class of medical practitioners exists, namely, the apothecaries. Prior to the days of Henry VIII. an apothecary seems to have been the common name in England for a general practitioner in medicine. About that time shops began to be established for the exclusive sale of drugs and medicinal compounds, and those who kept these shops often took upon them to doctor their customers. In 1542 Henry's parliament permitted any irregular practitioner to administer outward medicines, and these shopkeepers readily availed themselves of the permission granted by the Act and pushed the sale of their drugs and obtained larger prices on account of the advice they gave with them, and they appropriated exclusively the title of apothecaries. In 1617 they were incorporated under the name of "The Master, Wardens and Society of the Art and Mystery of Apothecaries of the City of London." About the beginning of the seventeenth century they began to prescribe as well as supply medicine; and although the College of Physicians resisted this poaching on what they considered their preserves, still early in the eighteenth century the matter was settled in favor of the apothecaries, since which time they have been legally recognised as a branch of the medical profession (*d*).

An Act of 1815 now regulates the practice of apothecaries throughout England and Wales, and no one can act as such or recover any charges for his services unless he has a certificate from the Society of Apothecaries. An apothecary is bound to make up any prescription duly signed by a licensed physician (*e*). Creswell, J., considered an apothecary one "who professes to judge of internal disease by his symptoms, and applies himself to cure that disease by medicine." And Glenn says that the practice of an apothecary may now be said to consist in attending and advising patients afflicted with diseases requiring medical (as distingushed from surgical) treatment; and prescribing, compounding and supplying medicines for their cure and relief (*f*).

The invention of medicine was generally attributed by the ancients to the gods, and both in Egypt and Greece female divinities were intimately connected with the healing art. Isis not only caused, but cured disease; she discovered—so it was said—many remedies and as late as Galen several compounds in the materia medica bore her name. Hygeia, the daughter of Æsculapius, was deemed

(*d*) *Rose* v. *Coll. of Phy.*, 3 Salk. 17 : 6 Mod. 44.
(*e*) 55 Geo. III. cap. 194. sec. 5.
(*f*) *Apoth. Co.* v. *Lotinga*, 2 Moo. & R. 499; Glenn's Laws Affecting Medical Men, p. 207.

the goddess of health, and Juno presided at accouchments. These fables show that in the remotest antiquity woman practised medicine. The laws of Greece, at a later period, forbad women to practise; thus, also, was it in Rome. However, 300 years before Christ, Agnodice—a young Athenian—dared to attend in disguise the schools of medicine forbidden to her sex. Preserving her incognito, when her education was finished she soon acquired a lucrative practice; and eventually her case caused the law against women to be revoked.

In the Middle Ages, among Mohammedans, many women were skilled in attending to the needs of their own sex; and among the Christians, nuns as well as monks ministered to bodies as well as souls diseased, practising both surgery and physic. In Italy, at Salerno, women prepared drugs and cosmetics, practised among persons of both sexes, took doctor's degrees, wrote treatises on medical subjects, obtained the royal authority to engage in the art, and composed poems in praise of their science. At the University of Bologna, as late as 1760, Anna Morandi Manzolini filled the chair of Anatomy; her reputation was European, and her lecture-room was frequented by students of all countries —so great was her skill in delicate dissections, and so clearly did she demonstrate the wonders of the human form divine. Dr. Maria delle Donne was professor of medicine and obstetrics in the same college in 1799; and many were the lady graduates of the Universities of Padua, Pavia and Ferrara, as well as Bologna.

In France, the earliest official document extant relative to the profession (dated 1311) forbids the practice of surgeons, or female surgeons, who have failed to pass the required examinations; and an edict of 1352 refers to female practitioners. In Spain, the Universities of Cordova, Salamanca and Alcala bestowed doctor's degrees on many women. In Germany, also, a number of the fair sex successfully cultivated the science of medicine, and practised it, in the last century and in the early part of this. In England, as has already been seen, in early days women practised the healing arts. Henry VIII. checked them for a time, but in his old age, changing his mind on this, as on almost every other subject, gave them liberty to minister to the outward and less serious ailments of his people.

Crossing the Atlantic an entry is found, under the date of March, 1638, which tells a tale. It is this: "Jane Hawkins, the wife of Richard Hawkins, had liberty till the beginning of the third month, called May, and the magistrates (if she did not depart before) to dispose of her: and in the meantime she is not to meddle in surgery or phisick, drinks, plaisters or oyles, nor to question matters of religion, except with the elders for satisfaction (g)." But now woman is no longer regarded as too good or too stupid to study medicine in America; in nearly every State in the Union she has free access to Medical Colleges (h). The Council of the College of Physicians and Surgeons of Ontario admit to registration and practice any person who complies with their requirements, without regard to sex. And the Imperial Parliament, by an Act passed in 1876, affirmed the principle that women are entitled to become registered practitioners of medicine.

(g) True Blue Laws of Connecticut, by J. H. Trumbull, 1876.
(h) Prof. H. C. Bolton, *Pop. Sci. Monthly*, vol. 18 p. 191.

## CHAPTER II.

### FEES.

The Roman Law considered the services of an advocate and of a physician as strictly honorific; and, as in the Roman age, practitioners in law and medicine, were usually men of leisure and wealthy, who did not practise for the sake of a livelihood, remuneration for their services could not be recovered in the ordinary way. Although owing to the Utopian ideas concerning the honour of a liberal profession then in vogue it was considered that any mention of a "fee," or a "salary," by that name would soil and disgrace the robe of a practitioner, still it was an established fiction of the Civil Law that the promise of an *honorarium* always accompanied the employment of a professional man, and that such promise created one of those obligations that might be enforced by action (*a*). The Common Law of England adopted the theory of the Civil Law as to the high standing of the profession, but afforded no remedy for the recovery of the charges. Surgeons and apothecaries were enabled to recover by law remuneration for their services, but a physician was presumed to attend his patient for an *honorarium* (something left to the honour of the patient to pay or not to pay), and could not maintain an action for his fees until the passing of the Medical Act, 1858, put an end to his anomalous position in this money-making age, and gave him as free an entrance into the courts of law to recover compensation for his work and labour, time and

---

(*a*) 3 Ortolan, Expli. des Instituts, sec. 1199, quoted in Ordronaux's Jurisprudence of Medicine.

skill bestowed, as the worker in any other path of life. Before this a physician could not recover even expenses out of pocket, such as those incurred in travelling to visit a patient, unless there had been an agreement specially made to that effect (*b*).

If a physician was a surgeon as well, and attended a case where the advice of a physician and the aid of a surgeon were necessary, he could recover the value of his services as a surgeon but not as a physician (*c*).

In England the question sometimes arises, where the practitioner is only a surgeon, whether he can charge for attendance as a physician or as an apothecary. It has been held that typhus fever is not a disease that belongs to a surgeon's branch of medicine, and that he cannot therefore recover for his attendance on a patient suffering under it. So, too, with regard to consumption and dropsy, though, in the latter case, he may recover for any work done for the patient specifically within his practise, such as puncturation, scarification, bandaging and friction (*d*).

At one time it was considered that an apothecary was not entitled to charges for his attendances, but only for his medicine: then the law decided that he might charge for either attendances or medicines, but not for both. Shortly afterwards Tenterden held that one might recover for attendance (the charge being reasonable), as well as for medicine. After that full justice was done to this branch of the profession, and it was decided that there was no rule of law, and there certainly is none of morals, to prevent an apothecary from making distinct charges for

(*b*) *Poucher* v. *Norman*, 3 B. & C. 744; *Chorley* v. *Bolcot*, 4 T. R. 317; *Veitch* v. *Russell*, 3 Q. B. 928.

(*c*) *Battersby* v. *Lawrence*, Car. & M. 277.

(*d*) Per *Bramwell, B.*; *Ellis* v. *Kelly*, 6 H. & N. 226; *Allison* v. *Haydon*, 3 C. & P. 246; *Apothecaries Co.* v. *Lotinga*, 2 Moo. & R. 495; *Battersby* v. *Lawrence*, Car. & M. 277.

attendances and medicines; but if he charges very high for his drugs the jury may think the attendances ought not to be paid for as well (*e*).

In Scotland, also, at one time physicians' fees were regarded as honoraries, and not recoverable by action except under a special contract (*f*). Neither in the United States nor in the Colonies have these distinctions been made between the different branches of the profession, nor has the principle been adopted that the profession of a physician is a merely honorary one, and that his services cannot be charged for (*g*).

In England every person registered according to the Medical Act, 1858, and in Ontario those registered under the Provincial Act, can practise medicine or surgery, or medicine and surgery; and can recover in any court of law, with full costs of suit, reasonable charges for professional aid, advice, and visits, and the costs of any medicine or other medical and surgical appliances rendered or supplied to his patient; but no person is entitled to recover any such charges in any court of law unless he can prove upon the trial that he is so registered. Registration has now become a part of the plaintiff's title to recover, which it is imperative upon him to prove. A copy of the medical register for the time being, purporting to be printed and published under the direction of the General Council, is evidence in all courts that the persons therein specified are registered according to the provisions of the Medical Act; and the absence of the name of any person is evidence, until the contrary be made to appear, that such person is not so registered; and the contrary may be shown by a certified copy, under the hand

---

(*e*) *Gensham* v. *Germain*, 11 Moore 1; *Towne* v. *Gresley*, 3 C. & P. 581; *Handey* v. *Henson*, 4 C. & P. 110; *Morgan* v. *Hallen*, 8 Ad. & E. 489.

(*f*) Stair I. 12; 5.

(*g*) *Adams* v. *Stevens*, 26 Wend. 451.

of the registrar, of the entry of the name of such person on the register (*h*). Similar rules are in force in the various States where Medical Boards have been constituted by legislative authorities for the purpose of examining and licensing practitioners, such as Alabama, Delaware, Florida, Georgia, Louisiana, Maine, Minnesota, New York, Ohio, South Carolina and Wisconsin.

Subject to the various statutory enactments, every physician or surgeon, or any one who chooses to act as such, is entitled to a reasonable reward for his services and for his medicines. If there was no express promise to pay when the services were requested, the law implies one: the broad principle being, that when a person has bestowed his skill and labor for the benefit of another, at his request, and no agreement is made in respect to them, the law raises an implied promise to pay such compensation as the person performing the service deserved to have; and when there is no statutory or other restraint upon the remedy, an action lies on such promise (*i*). The amount, unless settled by law, is a question for the jury, and in settling that, the eminence of the practitioner, the wealth of the patient, the delicacy and difficulty of the operation, as well as the time and care expended, are to be considered (*j*).

The law, as a rule, sets no limitation to fees, provided they be reasonable. Within this rule a practitioner is allowed discretionary powers and may charge more or less according to his own estimate of the value of his services. No one will pretend to assert that all services are of equal value, and no one will claim that those who can

(*h*) 21 & 22 Vict. cap. 90, sec. 27; *Simpson* v. *Dismore*, 9 M. & W. 47; R. S. Ont. cap. 142, secs. 35-36.

(*i*) *Hewitt* v. *Wilcox*, 1 Met. 154.

(*j*) *Adams* v. *Stevens*, 26 Wend. 451; *Baxter* v. *Gray*, 4 Scott, N. R. 374; *Mock* v. *Kelly*, 3 Ala. 387; *Beckman* v. *Planter*, 15 Barb. 550; *McPherson* v. *Chedell*, 24 Wend. 15; *Simmons* v. *Means*, 8 Sm. & Marsh. 397; *Smith* v. *Watson*, 14 Vt. 322.

render them the most skilfully should receive only the same reward as those who can render them the least so. A medical man of great eminence may be considered reasonably entitled to a larger recompense than one who has not equal practice, after it has become publicly understood that he expects a larger fee, inasmuch as the party applying to him must be taken to have employed him with a knowledge of this circumstance (*k*). But doctors must not be unreasonable in their charges; as Lord Kenyon remarked, "Though professional men are entitled to a fair and liberal compensation for their assistance, there are certain claims which they affect to set up, which if unreasonable or improper, it is for the jury to control" (*l*). That a patient is a millionaire does not justify an extortionate charge. The French rule is to consider the gravity of the disease as well as the fortune and position of the patient in settling the remuneration of a physician (*m*).

The existence of an epidemic does not authorise the charging of exorbitant fees (*n*).

In some ages and countries the fees payable to medical practitioners have been fixed by law. In Persia, for instance, in ancient times the law said that "a physician shall treat a priest for a pious blessing, or a spell; the master of a house for a small draught animal; the lord of a district for a team of four oxen; and if he cure the mistress of a house a female ass shall be his fee." (Vendidad Farg. VII.) To take another instance, the medical men in attendance upon the old princes of Wales had their fees settled; for curing a slight wound, a surgeon received for payment the clothes of the injured person which had been stained with blood;

---

(*k*) Ordronaux, sec. 39; Willcocks on the Medical Profession, p. 111.

(*l*) *Tuson* v. *Batting*, 3 Esp. N. P. 192; *Baxter* v. *Gray*, 4 Scott, N. R. 374.

(*m*) Affaire Tallien Jour. du Palais, vol. 3; An. XI., XII. p. 210.

(*n*) *Collins* v. *Grady*, 13 Louis. An. 95; 2 Louis. 331.

and for curing a dangerous wound he had, in addition to the bloody clothing, board and lodging while in attendance, and 180 pence. In Egypt, according to Herodotus, practitioners were paid out of the public treasury, although they might also receive fees from their patients.

A medical man can also recover for the services rendered by his assistants or students; and that even though the assistant is unregistered (*o*). It is not necessary that there should be any agreed specified price, he will be allowed what is usual and reasonable (*p*).

The right of a medical man to recover his charges for professional services does not depend upon his effecting a cure, or on his services being successful, unless there is a special agreement to that effect. It does not depend upon the fortune of the case whether it be good or bad, but upon the skill, diligence and attention bestowed. For, as a general rule, a physician does not guarantee the success of his treatment; he knows that that depends upon a higher power. Still, some good must have resulted from his efforts. The rule appears to be that if there has been no beneficial service there shall be no pay; but if some benefit has been derived, though not to the extent expected, this shall go to the amount of the plaintiff's demand, leaving the defendant to his action for negligence (*q*). The practitioner must be prepared to show that his work was properly done, if that be disputed, in order to prove that he is entitled to his reward (*r*). Where the surgical implements employed in amputating an arm were a large butcher knife and a carpenter's sash-saw, it was held that the Court rightly charged the jury, that if the

(*o*) *People* v. *Monroe*, 4 Wend. 200; *Blogg* v. *Parkers*, Ry. & M. N. P. C. 125.
(*p*) Story on Bailments, sec. 375.
(*q*) *Farnsworth* v. *Garrard*, 1 Camp. 38; *Adler* v. *Buckley*, 1 Swan (Tenn.) 69; *Gallagher* v. *Thompson*, Wright (Ohio), 466.
(*r*) *Basten* v. *Butter*, 7 East, 479.

operation was of service, and the patient did well and recovered, the surgeon was entitled to compensation, though it was not performed with the highest degree of skill, or might have been performed more skilfully by others (*s*).

If a surgeon has performed an operation which might have been useful but has merely failed in the event, he is nevertheless, entitled to charge; but, if it could not have been useful in any event, he will have no claim on the patient (*t*). A medical man who has made a patient undergo a course of treatment which plainly could be of no service, cannot make it a subject of charge; but an apothecary who has simply administered medicines under the direction of a physician may recover for the same, however improper they may have been (*u*). If the physician has employed the ordinary degree of skill required of one in his profession, and has applied remedies fitted to the complaint and calculated to do good in general, he is entitled to his fees, although he may have failed in this particular instance, such failure being then attributable to some vice or peculiarity in the constitution of the patient, for which the medical man is not responsible (*v*).

It is the duty of a physician who is attending a patient infected with a contagious disease, when called upon to attend others not so infected, to take all such precautionary means experience has proved to be necessary to prevent its communication to them. When a physician who was told by a patient not to attend any infected with small-pox or his services would be dispensed with, failed to say that he was attending such a patient, and

(*s*) *Adler* v. *Buckley*, 1 Swan (Tenn.), 69.
(*t*) *Hill* v. *Featherstonhaugh*, 7 Bing. 574; *Seare* v. *Prentise*, 8 East, 350.
(*u*) *Duffit* v. *James*, cited *Baston* v. *Butter*, 7 East, 480; *Kannen* v. *McMullen*, 1 Peake, 85; *Bellinger* v. *Craigue*, 31 Barb. 534; *Long* v. *Morrison*, 14 Ind. 595.
(*v*) *Kannen* v. *McMullen*, 1 Peake, 83; *Hupe* v. *Phelps*, 2 Starkie, 424.

promised not to do so, but continued to attend, and did by want of proper care communicate small-pox to the plaintiff and his family; it was held that these facts were proper evidence to go to the jury in reduction of damages in an action for his account, and that the physician was responsible in damages for the suffering, loss of time and damage to which the plaintiff may have been subjected. If a physician by communicating an infectious disease has rendered a prolonged attendance necessary, thereby increasing his bill, he cannot recover for such additional services necessitated by his own want of care (*w*). This rule will apply with equal force to puerperal fever (*x*).

In the case of vaccination, the physician, while he does not guarantee the specific value of the vaccine virus, yet guarantees its freshness; so that if he inoculate a patient with virus in an altered state, constituting as it then would mere putrid animal matter, and erysipelas or any injury to any limb necessitating amputation should arise, he will undoubtedly be held responsible for the suffering, loss of time, and permanent injury to the patient (*y*). Long since Lord Kenyon was of the opinion that if a surgeon was sent for to extract a thorn, which might be pulled out with a pair of nippers, and through his misconduct it became necessary to amputate the limb, the surgeon could not come into a court of justice to recover fees for the cure of the wound which he himself had caused (*z*).

The physician when sending in his bill should be specific in his charges and not general; he should give the number of visits and dates. In one case a lump charge of "$13 for medicine and attendance on one of the general's daughters

---

(*w*) *Piper* v. *Menifee*, 12 B. Monr. 467.
(*x*) Ordronaux p. 92.
(*y*) *Landon* v. *Humphrey*, 9 Conn. 209.
(*z*) Peake's N. P. C. 83, 84.

in curing the whooping cough," being objected to by the valiant officer, was held by the Court to be too loose to sustain an action (a). Where a practitioner brought an action for a bill consisting of a great number of items, and gave evidence as to some of them only, and the jury gave a verdict for the whole amount of the bill, the Court refused to interfere and grant a new trial because every item was not proved (b). Where a medical man delivered his bill to a patient without a specific charge, leaving a blank for his attendance, the Court inferred that he considered his demand in the light of a "*quiddam honorarium*," (this was before the Medical Act), and intended to leave it to the generosity of the patient, and the latter having paid into court a certain amount, the Court held the surgeon was bound by the amount so paid and could not recover any more (c). As a rule, however, if a doctor's bill is not paid when presented he is not limited by it to the amount of his claim, if he can show that his services were of greater value (d). When witnesses are called to speak as to the value of the practitioner's services the Courts generally incline towards the lowest estimate (e).

The number of visits required must depend on each particular case, and the physician is deemed the best and proper judge of the necessity of frequent visits; and in the absence of proof to the contrary, the Court will presume that all the professional visits made were deemed necessary and were properly made (f). There must not be too many *consultations*; and the physician called in for consultation or to perform an operation may recover his fees from the

(a) *Hughes* v. *Hampton*, Const. Rep. (S. C.) 745.
(b) *Wheeler* v. *Sims*, 5 Jur. 151; *Newton* v. *Ker*, 14 Louis. An. 704.
(c) *Tuson* v. *Batting*, 3 Esp. 191.
(d) *Miller* v. *Beal*, 26 Ind. 234.
(e) *Collins* v. *Graves*, 13 Louis. An. 95; *Villalobas* v. *Mooney*, 2 Louis. 331.
(f) *Todd* v. *Myers*, 40 Cal. 357.

patient, notwithstanding that the attending practitioner summoned him for his own benefit and had arranged with the patient that he himself would pay (*g*).

Where a medical man has attended as a friend, he cannot charge for his visits. This was held in one case where it was proved that the practitioner had attended the patient as a friend, upon the understanding that he was to have refreshments and dinners free of charge; and in another case, where a medical man had attended professionally, for several years, a lady with whom he was on terms of intimacy (but received no fees, except once, when he had prescribed for her servant). The day before her death this lady had written to her executors, asking them to remunerate the doctor in a handsome manner, and moreover in her will she gave him a legacy of £3,000 and a reversionary interest in £6000 more. It was proved that he had attended others without having taken fees or sent in bills. It was held that his services had been tendered as for a friend, and accepted as a friend, and his demand as a debt against the assets of the lady was rejected (*h*). One would have thought that the physician in this latter case should have been satisfied.

Where a tariff of fees has been prepared, and agreed to by the physicians in any locality, they are bound by it legally as far as the public is concerned, morally as far as they themselves are concerned (*i*). It is no part of the physicians business to supply the patient with drugs; if he does so he has a right to be reimbursed therefor (*j*).

---

(*g*) *Succession of Duclos*, 11 Louis. An. 406; *Sheldon* v. *Johnson*, 40 Ia. 84; *Guerard* v. *Jenkins*, 1 Strobh. 171; Ordronaux, sec. 47.

(*h*) *Roberts* v. *Kerfoot*, cited Glenn's Laws, p. 201; *Stackman* v. *Vivian*, 84 Beav. 290.

(*i*) Ordronaux, sec. 43.

(*j*) *Bassett* v. *Spofford*, 11 N. H. 167.

If a physician enters into a special contract to perform a cure he will be held strictly to its terms, nor will he be allowed to plead circumstances, which, under the general law of professional obligation, might fairly exonerate him from blame, for failing of success in the treatment of his patient. To promise an absolute cure is to assume arrogantly the possession of powers never delegated to man; only a weak and vapid intellect will commit so egregious a blunder. Yet, if a man choose to do it he may, and having entered into an *express* contract he will be held liable for its fulfilment. For it is his own fault if he undertake a thing above his strength. If the agreement is, no cure, no pay: he cannot even recover for medicines supplied if the cure is not effected. At least, so it was held at Vermont. Contracts to receive a certain sum contingent upon the performance of a cure have always been considered as professionally immoral, and in the civil law were repudiated as against public policy (*k*).

The physician is always allowed discretionary powers over the patient entrusted to his care in modes of treatment, so as to be able to alter them according to the varying necessities of the case. Unless such change of treatment involves a risk of life or consequences of which he is unwilling to assume the responsibility, he is not under obligation to give notice or obtain permission before making it. Particularly is this the case where the patient is not at home or among friends or relatives, but is in some degree in his custody and under his exclusive supervision, as well as care. In such circumstances he is authorised to perform operations, or change his treatment, or enforce discipline essential to its fulfilment, without first consulting or obtaining permission from friends or guardians at a distance, since delay might involve a greater risk to the health

(*k*) *Smith* v. *Hyde*, 19 Verm. 54; *Mock* v. *Kelly*, 3 Alab. 387; Jones on Bailm. 99; Ordronaux, secs. 21 and 15.

and possibly the life of the patient than would a necessitated operation; and of such things he alone is the proper, as he alone can be the best, judge. He may recover his fees for such operation or change of treatment without proving that it was necessary or proper, or that before he performed it he gave notice to the party who had to pay, or that it would have been dangerous to have waited until such notice had been given. The burden of proving unskilfulness or carlessness in the operation lies upon the party objecting to it (*l*).

When a medical man is called as a witness before a court, to testify as to facts within his knowledge, he must attend and give evidence upon payment of the same fees as other witnesses are entitled to; unless it is otherwise provided by statute.

Where a statute provides that a medical man should be paid a certain witness fee, he is entitled to that fee although he be not called to give professional evidence, and it is not necessary to prove that he is in practice (*m*). A witness should be paid his fees when he is subpœnaed; but even if he attends he can refuse to give evidence until he is paid, unless he takes the oath before making the objection (*n*). A subpœna should be served a reasonable time before the trial, to enable a witness to put his affairs in such order that his attendance on the court may be as little detrimental as possible to his interests (*o*).

Where a medical man is summoned to attend a coroner's inquest, unless the statute law is clearly to the contrary,

---

(*l*) *McClallen* v. *Adams*, 19 Pick. 333; Ordronaux, sec. 48.

(*m*) *Parkinson* v. *Atkinson*, 31 L. J., C. P. 199; *Turner* v. *Turner*, 5 Jur., N. S., 839.

(*n*) *Clark* v. *Gill*, 1 Kay & J. 19; *Webb* v. *Paige*, 1 Car. & Kir. 23.

(*o*) *Hammond* v. *Stewart*, 1 Stra. 510.

he is only entitled to be paid for each days attendance, not for each body on which the inquest was held (*p*).

Under the Ontario Act, R. S. cap. 79, a coroner, if he finds that the deceased was attended during his last illness, or at his death, by a duly qualified medical man, may summon that medical man to attend the inquest; if he finds that he was not so attended, he may summons any legally qualified neighbouring practitioner, and may direct him to hold a post-mortem examination; but a second practitioner will not be entitled to any fees, unless a majority of the jury have, in writing, asked him to be called (*q*). The fees are, for attendance without *post-mortem* $5, if with *post-mortem*, without an analysis of the contents of the stomach or intestines, $10; if with such analysis, $20; together with a mileage each way of twenty cents. If the practitioner when duly summoned fails to attend, without sufficient reason, he is liable to a penalty of $40 (*r*).

Is an expert witness entitled to receive greater compensation than an ordinary witness? or can he be compelled to give a professional opinion without being paid for it? The States of Iowa, North Carolina and Rhode Island have answered these questions by statutes which say such witnesses shall be entitled to extra compensation to be fixed by the court, in its discretion: while Indiana says experts may be compelled to appear and testify to opinions without payment or tender of compensation other than the *per diem* and mileage allowed by law to other witnesses (*s*).

The subject does not appear to have been very much considered in England. In a case, at *Nisi Prius*, Lord

(*p*) *In re Askin & Charteris*, 13 U. C. R. 498.
(*q*) *In re Harbottle & Wilson*, 30 U. C. R. 314.
(*r*) R. S. O. cap. 79, sec. 10.
(*s*) Iowa Code, 1873, sec. 1814; North Carolina Laws, 1871, cap. 139, sec. 13; Rhode Is. Pub. Stat. 1882, p. 733; Indiana Rev. Stat. 1881, p. 94, sec. 504.

Campbell declared that an expert was not bound to attend upon being served with a subpœna, and that he ought not to be subpœnaed; that he could not be compelled to attend to speak merely to matters of opinion (*t*). And Mr. Justice Maule, where an expert demanded additional compensation, said there was a distinction between a witness to facts and a witness selected by a party to give his opinion on a subject with which he is peculiarly conversant from his employment in life. The former is bound as a matter of public duty to testify as to all facts within his knowledge, the latter is under no such obligation, and the party who selects him must pay him for his time before he will be compelled to give evidence (*u*).

Worden, J., of the Supreme Court of Indiana, in considering the question, in a case that came up prior to the statute above referred to, reviewed most of the American decisions and the opinions of the text writers, and concluded " that physicians and surgeons, whose opinions are valuable to them as a source of their income and livelihood, cannot be compelled to perform service by giving such opinions in a court of justice without payment." The Court further said, " It would seem, on general principles, that the knowledge and learning of a physician should be regarded as his property, which ought not to be extorted from him in the form of opinions without just compensation." " If the professional services of a lawyer cannot be required in a civil or criminal case without compensation, how can the professional services of a physician be thus required? Is not his medical knowledge his capital stock? Are his professional services more at the mercy of the public than the services of a lawyer? When a physician testifies as an expert by giving his opinion, he is performing a strictly

(*t*) *Belts* v. *Clifford*, Warwick Assizes, Lent, 1858.
(*u*) *Webb* v. *Paige*, 1 Car. & Ker. 23.

professional service. * * * The position of a medical witness testifying as an expert is much more like that of a lawyer than that of an ordinary witness testifying to facts. The purpose of this service is not to prove facts in the cause, but to aid the Court or Jury in arriving at a proper conclusion from facts otherwise proved " (*v*).  In an earlier case (in 1854), in Massachusetts, the Court said, " to compel a person to attend because he is accomplished in a particular science, art or profession, would subject the same individual to be called upon in every case in which any question in his department of knowledge is to be solved. Thus, the most eminent physician might be compelled, merely for the ordinary witness fees, to attend from the remotest part of the district, and give his opinion in every trial in which a medical question should arise. This is so unreasonable that nothing but necessity can justify it" (*w*).

On a trial for murder the prosecution had procured the attendance of Dr. Hammond to testify professionally, and had agreed to give him $500 as his fee. This fee was complained of as an irregularity, but the Court in delivering judgment remarked, " The district attorney, it is true, might have required the attendance of Dr. H. on subpœna, but that would not have sufficed to qualify him as an expert with clearness and certainty upon the questions involved. He would have met the requirements of the subpœna if he had appeared in court when he was required to testify and given impromptu answers to such questions as might have been put to him. He could not have been required, under process of subpœna, to examine the case, and to have used his skill and knowledge to enable him to give an opinion upon any points of the case, nor to have attended during the whole trial and attentively considered and carefully

---

(*v*) *Buchman* v. *State*, 59 Ind. 1.
(*w*) In *Re Roelker*. 1 Sprague, 276.

heard all the testimony given on both sides, in order to qualify him to give a deliberate opinion upon such testimony, as an expert, in respect to the question of the sanity of the prisoner;" and held " that there was no irregularity in the payment of such a fee " (*x*).

Such text writers of high repute as Taylor, Phillips, Redfield and Ordronaux, all agree that an expert cannot be compelled to give professional opinions without proper remuneration. The last named writer says, "Where a subpœna is served upon an expert he must obey it, if within the range of physical possibility. But once on the stand as a skilled witness his obligation to the public ceases, and he stands in the position of any professional man consulted in relation to a subject upon which his opinion is sought. He cannot be compelled to bestow his skill and professional experience gratuitously; whoever calls for an opinion from him in chief must pay him, and the expert may decline to answer until the party calling him has paid. When he has given his evidence he cannot decline repeating it, or explaining it. A similar rule will, by parity of reasoning, apply to personal services demanded from the expert, as well as to opinions asked " (*y*).

On the other hand, the Supreme Court of Alabama, in 1875 (*z*), confirmed a fine imposed upon a physician for refusing to state the nature and character of a wound received by a man and its probable effect, upon the ground that he had not been remunerated for his professional opinion, nor had compensation for it been promised or secured. And the Court of Appeals in Texas, in 1879, held, that the court could compel a physician to testify as to the

---

(*x*) *People* v. *Montgomery*, 13 Abb. Pr. (N. S.), 207.
(*y*) Juris. of Med. secs. 114-116; 1 Tay. Med. Jur. p. 19; 2 Phil. Ev. 4th Am. Ed., p. 828; 1 Redf. on Wills, pp. 154-155.
(*z*) Exparte *Dement*, 53 Ala. 389.

result of a post-mortem examination; adding, that a medical expert could not be compelled to make a post-mortem examination unless paid for it, but an examination having already been made by him he could be obliged to disclose the results thereof (a).

The result of the authorities seems to be that, without the aid of a statute, an expert cannot be compelled to bestow his skill and professional experience gratuitously upon any party, for his skill and experience are his individual capital and property.

(a) *Summer* v. *State*, 5 Tex. Ct. of App. 574.

## CHAPTER III.

### WHO SHOULD PAY THE DOCTOR.

If Smith says to Brown, a medical man, "Attend upon Robinson, and if he does not pay you I will;" that being a promise to answer for a debt of Robinson's, for which he is also liable, the guarantee is only a collateral undertaking, and, under the Statute of Frauds, must be in writing and signed by Smith, or some other person thereunto by him lawfully authorised, in order to be binding upon him. But if Smith says to Dr. Brown, absolutely and unqualifiedly, "Attend upon Robinson, and charge your bill to me," or "I will pay you for your attendance upon Robinson;" then the whole credit being given to Smith, no written agreement is necessary to enable the doctor to recover the amount of his account from him, since it is absolutely the debt of Smith (a).

Where a person calls at the office of a physician, and, he being absent, the visitor leaves his business card with these words written on it, "Call on Mrs. Jones, at No. 769 High Street," handing it to the clerk in attendance, with the request that he would give it to the doctor and tell him to go as soon as possible; this caller becomes liable to pay the doctor's bill for attendance upon Mrs. Jones in pursuance of such message. Yet Mrs. Jones, if a widow, may also be liable; for one who acquiesces in the employment of a physician, and implies, by his or her conduct, that the doctor is attending at his or her request, is responsible for

---

(a) Smith on Contracts, 85.

the value of his services. If Mrs. Jones is living with her husband, or, without her fault, away from him, the doctor has still another string to his bow, and may recover the amount of his bill from Mr. Jones; for the rule is, that a husband must pay his wife's doctor's bills. Of course the doctor cannot make all three pay (b).

Long since, Park, J., was clearly of the opinion that if a mere stranger directed a surgeon to attend a poor man, such person was clearly liable to pay the surgeon (c). Yet, in some cases in the United States, it has been held that the man who merely calls the doctor is not bound to pay him. When, for instance, in Pennsylvania, a son of full age, when living with his father, fell sick, and the father went for the doctor, urging him to visit his son. Afterwards the physician sued the parent. The Court said this was wrong, that he should have sued the son, as the father went as a messenger only, that the son, who had the benefit of the services, was the responsible person; and remarked that it was clear that had the defendant been a stranger, however urgent he may have been and whatever opinions the physician may have formed as to his liability, he would not have been chargeable without an express promise to pay, as, for instance, in the case of an inn-keeper or any other individual whose guest may receive the aid of medical service. A different principle, the Court considered, would be very pernicious, as but very few would be willing to run the risk of calling in the aid of a physician where the patient was a stranger or of doubtful ability to pay. This was in 1835 (d). And, in Vermont, one brother took another, who was insane, to a private lunatic asylum and asked that he (the insane one), might be taken in and

---

(b) *Bradley* v. *Dodge*, 45 How., N. Y., Pr. 57; *Craine* v. *Bandoine*, 65 Barb., N. Y., 261; *Harrison* v. *Grady*, 13 L. T., N. S., 369; *Spaun* v. *Mercer*, 8 Neb., 537.

(c) *Watling* v. *Walters*, 1 C. & P. 132.

(d) *Boyd* v. *Sappington*, 6 Watts, 247.

cared for. This was done. In course of time the doctor sued the sane one for his bill, but the Court would not aid him in the matter, saying, "He is not liable unless he promised to pay" *(e)*.

In the case of Mr. Dodge, above referred to, the Court said, "He might very readily have screened himself from all liability, by simply writing the memorandum on a blank card, or by adding to that which he wrote on his own card something that would have apprised the doctor of the fact that he acted in the matter for Mrs. Jones, as her agent."

The reporter did not approve of this decision, and so appended the following graphic note: "Let us see how this thing works. We will take as an illustration an almost every-day occurrence arising in the country. A. B. is taken suddenly and seriously ill in the night time, and sends to his neighbour, C. D. living in the next house to his, to have him go after the doctor as soon as he can, for he is in great pain and distress. C. D. jumps out of bed without hesitation, and hastily dresses himself, and goes out to his barn and takes a horse from the stable, and not waiting to put on a saddle or bridle, jumps on to the horse with the halter only, puts him at full speed for the doctor's office, some two or three miles distant. On arriving there he finds the doctor absent from home, but his clerk is there, and C. D. at once says, 'Tell the doctor to call on A. B. who has been taken suddenly sick; tell him to come as soon as possible.' In accordance with this message the doctor calls upon A. B., and prescribes for and attends him professionally for several days. After a reasonable time the doctor sends in his bill to A. B. and it not being paid as soon as the doctor desires, he calls on C. D. and requests him to pay the bill. C. D. with perfect astonishment, asks why he is to pay.

*(e) Smith v. Watson,* 14 Vt. 332.

The doctor informs him that he made himself liable to pay the bill because, when he delivered the message, he did not tell the clerk that he came for the doctor by the request of A. B. nor that he acted as agent of A. B. in delivering his message. Well, says C. D. the fact was I did go at the request of A. B. and merely acted as his agent in delivering the message, and I will swear to these facts if necessary. The doctor insists that it will do him no good if he should give such testimony, for the law is settled on that point, as just such a case has recently been decided in New York under just such a state of facts, where the jury, in the justice court, found a verdict for the doctor for the amount of his bill, and, on appeal by the defendant to the general term of the New York Common Pleas, that court unanimously sustained the verdict of the jury, and affirmed the judgment of the court below. Well, says C. D. 'If that is the law I think I will wait awhile before I go after a doctor again as an act of neighbourly kindness.'" This case was decided as late as March, 1873.

A wife has implied authority to bind her husband for reasonable expense incurred in obtaining medicines and medical attendance during illness; but this implied authority is put an end to if she commits adultery while living apart from her husband, and there has been no subsequent condonation; or, if she leaves her husband's home of her own accord and without sufficient reason, and the fact has become notorious, or the husband has given sufficient notice that he will no longer be responsible for any debts that she may incur (*f*). If a husband turn an innocent wife out of doors without the means of obtaining necessaries, it is a presumption of law, which cannot be rebutted by evidence, that she was turned out with the authority of her husband to pledge his credit for necessaries, and in such a case

(*f*) *Harrison* v. *Grady*, 13 L. T., N. S. 369; *Cooper* v. *Lloyd*, 6 C. B., N. S. 519; Roper on Husband and Wife, 2nd ed. v. ii. p. 114.

medical attendance will be considered as one of the primary necessaries (*g*). A married woman's misconduct does not exonerate the husband from paying a doctor whom he requests to attend her (*h*).

Although the law requires the husband to furnish the wife with all necessaries suitable to his condition in life, including medical attendance in case of sickness, still it gives him the right to procure these necessaries himself and to decide from whom and from what place they are to come. If a physician attends a wife whom he knows to be living separate and apart from her husband, he ought to enquire whether she has good cause for so doing; for if she has not he cannot make the husband pay the bill; and it has been held that it devolves upon the doctor to show that there was sufficient cause for the wife's separation (*i*). The employment of a physician by a husband to attend his sick wife, presumably continues throughout the illness; and the mere fact that the wife is removed, with the husband's consent, from his home to her father's, will not enable him to resist payment of the doctor's bill for visits paid to her at the father's (*j*).

Notwithstanding the law's desire not to favour any particular school, a quack's bill was thrown out where the services were rendered without the husband's assent. This was done in a case where a doctor was in the habit of putting a woman into a mesmeric sleep, she thereupon became a clairvoyant and prescribed the medicines which the doctor furnished, and for these he sued. The Judge said:—"The law does not recognize the dreams, visions or revelations of a woman in mesmeric sleep as necessaries for

---

(*g*) *Harrison* v. *Grady*, supra; *Thorpe* v. *Shapleigh*, 67 Me. 235.
(*h*) *Webber* v. *Spaunpake*, 2 Redf., N. Y., 258.
(*i*) *Berier* v. *Galloway*, 71 Ill. 517; *Hartmann* v. *Tegart*, 12 Kan. 177.
(*j*) *Potter* v. *Virgil*, 67 Barb. N. Y., 578.

a wife for which the husband, without his consent, can be made to pay. These are fancy articles which those who have money of their own to dispose of may purchase if they think proper, but they are not necessaries known to the law for which the wife can pledge the credit of the absent husband" (*k*).

In England, it was, until 1869, considered that a parent's duty to furnish necessaries for an infant child was a moral and not a legal one, so that he was not liable to pay for medicines or medical aid furnished to his child without some proof of a contract on his part either expressed or implied. And this still is the view where the child is over fourteen. The rule of law varies in the different States of the Union. In most of those in which the question has come before the courts the legal liability of the parent for necessaries furnished to the infant is asserted, unless they are otherwise supplied by the father; and it is put upon the ground that the moral obligation is a legal one, and some of the courts have declared this quite strongly. In other States the old English rule has been held to be law, and agency and authority have been declared to be the only ground of such liability. The authority of the infant to bind the parent for medical aid supplied him will be inferred from very slight evidence (*l*). But a contract to pay will not be implied when the infant has been allowed a sufficiently reasonable sum for his expenses (*m*). Where the services have been rendered with the parent's knowledge and consent, he will generally have to pay for them. A boy left home against his father's will, and refused to return at his parent's command. Being seized with a mortal illness he did at last come back. His father went with him to a phy-

---

(*k*) *Wood* v. *O'Kelley*, 8 Cush. 406.

(*l*) Parsons on Contracts, vol. i. p. 302-303; *Blackburn* v. *Mackey*, 1 C. & P. 1.

(*m*) *Crantz* v. *Gill*, 2 Esp. 471.

sician to obtain medical advice, and the doctor afterwards visited him professionally at his father's house. No express promise to pay was proved, nor had the father said he would not pay. The Court held the father liable to pay the doctor's bill (*n*). And in an English case, where a father had several of his children living at a distance from his own house under the protection of servants, it was held that if an accident happened to one of the children he was liable to pay for the medical attendance on such child, although he might not know the surgeon called in, and although the accident might have been received through the carelessness of a servant (*o*).

By a recent English statute (*p*), when any parent shall wilfully neglect to provide adequate food, clothing, medical aid, or lodging for his child, in his custody, under the age of fourteen, whereby the child's health shall have been, or shall be likely to be, seriously injured, he shall be guilty of an indictable offence punishable by imprisonment. Charles Downes was the two-year-old child of a member of the sect of Peculiar People. These people never call in medical aid or give medicines: to do so would be contrary to their religious opinions; but if any is sick they call in the elders of the church, who pray over him, anointing him with oil in the name of the Lord; then they hope for a cure, as they have thus literally complied with the directions in the 14th and 15th verses of the 5th chapter of the Epistle of St. James. This child was ill for months; the usual course was pursued by his father; no medical aid was obtained, although easily obtainable. The illness was misunderstood, and, although he was taken care of and well supplied with food, the child died. The father was indicted for manslaughter, and the

(*n*) *Rogers* v. *Turner*, 59 Mo. 116; *Deane* v. *Annis*, 14 Me. 26; *Swain* v. *Tyler*, 26 Vt. 1.
(*o*) *Cooper* v. *Phillips*, 4 C. & P. 581.
(*p*) 31 & 32 Vict. cap. 122, sec. 37.

jury found that the death was caused by the neglect to obtain medical assistance, that the father *bona fide* (though erroneously) believed that medical aid was not required, and that it was wrong to use it. The Judge entered a verdict of guilty, and the Court held—under this statute—that a positive duty was imposed upon the father to provide adequate medical aid when necessary, whatever his conscientious scruples might be, and that that duty having been wilfully neglected by the prisoner, and death having ensued from that neglect, he was properly convicted of manslaughter *(q)*.

It had been held by Pigott, B., in a case against these same Peculiar People, and also by Willis, J., that, at common law, there was no legal duty upon a father to employ a physician for his sick child *(r)*.

It is not enough to shew neglect of reasonable means for preserving or prolonging the child's life, to convict of manslaughter, it must be shewn that the neglect had the effect of shortening life. It will not do merely to prove that proper medical aid might have saved or prolonged life and would have increased the chance of recovery, but that it might have been of no avail *(s)*. In this case the father, perhaps, might have been convicted of neglect of duty as a parent, under the statute (per Stephen, J.).

Medicines and medical aid are necessaries for which an infant may legally contract, and for which he can render himself liable. In Massachusetts, it was held that he would not be liable merely because his father was poor and unable to pay *(t)*.

(q) *Reg.* v. *Downes,* 1 Q. B. D. 25.

(r) *Reg.* v. *Hines,* 80 Cen. C. C. Sess. Pap. 309; *Reg.* v. *Wagstaffe,* 10 Cox. C. C. 530.

(s) *Reg.* v. *Morby,* 8 Q. B. D. 571.

(t) *Blackburn* v. *Mackey,* 1 C. & P. 1; *Hoyt* v. *Casey,* 14 Mass. 397.

A master is not bound to provide medical assistance for his servant, but the obligation, if it exists at all, must arise from contract; nor will such a contract be implied simply because the servant is living under the master's roof, nor because the illness of the servant has arisen from an accident met with in the master's service (*u*). But where a servant left in charge of her master's children was made ill by suckling one of the children, and called in a medical man to attend her, with the knowledge and without the disapprobation of her mistress, it was decided that the doctor could make the father and master pay (*v*). And a master is bound to provide an apprentice with proper medicines and medical attendance (*w*).

In England, when a pauper meets with an accident, the parish where it occurs is usually liable for the surgeon's bill. If, however, the illness of the pauper arises from any other cause than accident or sudden calamity, the parish in which he is settled is under legal liability to supply him with medical aid, although he may be residing in another parish. But all these questions with regard to paupers are determined according to the poor laws of the different countries(*x*).

It has frequently happened that when a railway passenger or employee has been injured by a collision or accident, and some railway official has called in a doctor, the company has afterwards refused to pay the bill; and the courts have declined to make them do so, unless it be shown that the agent or servant who summoned the medical man had authority to do so. It has been held that neither a guard, nor the superintendent of a station, nor the engineer of the train in which the accident happened, had any implied authority, as incidental

---

(*u*) *Wennall* v. *Adney*, 3 B. & P. 24; *Sellen* v. *Norman*, 4 C. & P. 80.
(*v*) *Cooper* v. *Phillips*, 4 C. & P. 581.
(*w*) *R.* v. *Smith*, 8 C. & P. 153.
(*x*) Glenn's Law of Medical Men, pp. 197-199.

to their positions, to render their companies liable for medical services so rendered (*y*). The Court of Exchequer said, " It is not to be supposed that the result of their decision will be prejudicial to railway travellers who may happen to be injured. It will rarely occur that the surgeon will not have a remedy against his patient, who, if he be rich, must at all events pay; and if poor, the sufferer will be entitled to a compensation from the company, if they by their servants have been guilty of a breach of duty, out of which he will be able to pay, for the surgeon's bill is always allowed for in damages. There will, therefore, be little mischief to the interests of the passengers, little to the benevolent surgeons who give their services." But, in England, it has been decided that the general manager of a railway company has, as incidental to his employment, authority to bind his company for medical services bestowed upon one injured on his railway. In Illinois, a similar decision was given as to a general superintendent, although in New York judgment was given the other way (*z*).

If an accident happen to a stage coach by which a passenger's leg is broken, or his human form divine is otherwise injured, the coachman has no authority to bind his master by a contract with a surgeon to attend to the injury ; nor if a lamp-lighter, by neglect, burn any person, has he, or any officers of the gas company, power to bind the company by a contract for the cure of the injured person (*a*). If ordinary employees had such authority, then every servant who, by his negligence or misconduct, had caused injury to an individual, would have an implied authority to employ, on behalf and at the expense of his employer, any person he thought fit to remedy the mischief.

(*y*) *Cox* v. *Midland Counties Railway*, 3 Ex. 268; *Cooper* v. *N. Y. C.* 13 N. Y. Sup. Ct. 276.

(*z*) *Walker* v. *Great Western Railway*, 2 L. R. Ex. 228 ; *Cairo, etc., Railroad Company* v. *Mahoney*, 82 Ill. 73; *Stephenson* v. *N. Y. & H. R. R. Co.*, 2 Duer. 341.

(*a*) Per Parke, B., and Rolfe, B., in *Cox* v. *Mid. Co. Railway*, supra.

## CHAPTER IV.

### WHO MAY PRACTISE.

The law has nothing to do with the merits of particular systems or schools of medicine. Their relative merits may become the subject of inquiry when the skill or ability of a practitioner, in any given case, is to be passed upon as a matter of fact. But the law does not and cannot supply any positive rules for the interpretation of medical science. It is not one of those certain or exact sciences in which truths become established and fixed, but it is essentially progressive in its nature. No one system of practice has been uniformly followed, but physicians, from the days of Hippocrates, have been divided into opposing sects and schools. The sects of the dogmatists and the empirics divided the ancient world for centuries until the rise of the methodics, who in their turn gave way to innumerable sects. Theories of practice believed to be infallible in one age have been utterly rejected in another. For thirteen centuries Europe yielded to the authority of Galen. He was implicitly followed, his practice strictly pursued. Everything that seemed to conflict with his precepts was rejected; and yet, in the revolutions of medical opinion, the works of this undoubtedly great man were publicly burned by Paracelsus and his disciples; and for centuries following the medical world was divided between the Galenists and the chemists, until a complete ascendancy over both was obtained by the vitalists. This state of things has been occasioned by the circumstance that medical practitioners have often been more given to the formation of theories upon the nature of disease and the mode of its treatment, than to that careful observation and patient accumulation of facts by which, in other sciences, the phenomena of nature have been unravelled. \* \* \* It is not to be overlooked that as an art it has been characterised in a greater degree by fluctuations of opinion as to its principles and the mode of its practice than perhaps any other pursuit. That it has been distinguished by the constant promulgation and explosion of theories. That it has alternated between the advancement of new doctrines and the revival of old ones; and that its professors in every age have been noted for the tenacity with which they have clung to opinions, and the unanimity with which they have resisted the introduction of valuable discoveries. They still continue to disagree in respect to the treatment of diseases as old as the human race; and at the present day \* \* \* a radical and fundamental difference divides the allopathists from the followers of Hahnneman, to say nothing of those who believe in the sovereign instrumentality. \* \* \* The axiom that doctors differ is as true now as ever it was (*a*). Thus spake Daly, J.; the reporter observes in a note: " It may, perhaps, be safely questioned whether the sister sciences of law and theology present any such unity or certainty of opinion as might enable them to arraign the medical profession."

In Great Britain and Ireland, since the passing of the Medical Act of 1858, every one registered under the provisions of that Act is entitled, according to his qualification, to practise medicine or surgery, or both (as the case may be), in any part of Her Majesty's Dominions, and to recover on any court of law (should any patient neglect to pay) his reasonable charges for professional aid, advice and visits, and the costs of any medicine, or other medical or surgical appliances rendered or supplied by

---

(*a*) *Corsi v. Maretzek,* 4 E. D. Smith 1 (1855).

him to his patient; but any one not so registered cannot recover any such charges in any court of law. Proof of registration is absolutely necessary for a recovery; but it will suffice if the registration has taken place before the trial (*b*).

And as to who may be registered; the Act says any one may be who is a fellow, member, licentiate, or extra licentiate, of the Royal College of Physicians of London, or of the Royal College of Physicians of Edinburgh, or of the King and Queen's College of Ireland; or fellow, member, or licentiate in midwifery, of the Royal College of Surgeons of England, or fellow or licentiate of the Royal College of Surgeons of Edinburgh, or of the Faculty of Physicians and Surgeons of Glasgow, or of the Society of Apothecaries, London, or of the Apothecaries Hall, Dublin; or doctor, bachelor, or licentiate of medicine, of any university of the United Kingdom, or licentiate in surgery of any university in Ireland; or doctor of medicine by doctorate granted prior to August, 1858, by the Archbishop of Canterbury; or doctor of medicine of any foreign or colonial college, after examination, or who satisfies the Council of Education and Registration that there is sufficient reason for admitting him to be registered (*c*).

In France, the medical profession is divided into two grades; in the higher grade are all doctors of medicine of the universities; those in the lower grade are *officiers de santé*. In Germany, the right to practise is conferred by a state licence granted on passing the *staats-examen*: the degree of doctor of medicine is almost always taken at some university after obtaining the state license. In Austria, the

---

(*b*) 21 & 22 Vict. cap. 90, secs. 31, 32; *Wagstaffe* v. *Sharpe*, 3 M. & W. 521; *Shearwood* v. *Hay*, 5 Ad. & E. 383; *Turner* v. *Reynall*, 14 C. B. N. S. 328.

(*c*) 21 & 22 Vict. cap. 90, sec. 15.

right to practise is carried by the degree of doctor of medicine obtained from a university (d).

The legislature of every colony of Great Britain has full power to make laws for the purpose of enforcing the registration within its jurisdiction of medical practitioners, including those registered under the Imperial Act.

In Ontario, the medical profession is incorporated under the name and style of "The College of Physicians and Surgeons of Ontario," and every person registered under the provisions of the Ontario Medical Act (e) is a member of the college. There is a "Council," in part appointed by certain educational institutions, in part elected by practitioners. This council fixes the curriculum of studies, appoints examiners, and arranges the examinations of those desirous of admission to practise; it also arranges for the registration of those who pass the examinations, or had certain qualifications before July, 1870. Every one who passes the examinations and has complied with the rules and regulations of the council, and paid his fees, is entitled to registration, and by virtue thereof to practise medicine, surgery and midwifery in the Province. If registration is not granted to one he may compel it by a writ of mandamus (f).

Registration is essential to entitle a practitioner to recover any charges for medical or surgical advice, or for attendance, or for performance of any operation, or for any medicine he may have prescribed or supplied. (This last clause does not apply to any licensed chemist or druggist.) And if any one unregistered, for hire, gain or hope of reward, practises or professes to practise medicine, surgery or midwifery, or advertises to give advice therein, he is liable

(d) Enc. Brit. Vol. xv. p. 799.
(e) R. S. O. cap. 142.
(f) *Reg. v. Coll. Phy. & Sur.*, 44 Ont. Q. B. 564.

to a fine of from $25 to $100. And any one not registered who takes or uses any name, title, addition or description implying or calculated to lead people to infer that he is registered, or that he is recognized by law as a physician, surgeon, accoucheur, or a licentiate in medicine, surgery or midwifery, is liable to the same penalty. Any person who wilfully or falsely pretends to be a physician, doctor of medicine, surgeon, or general practitioner, or assumes any title, addition or description, other than he actually possesses and is legally entitled to, is liable to a fine of from $10 to $50. But it is not punishable to practise for love or charity, and any one who has the degree of doctor of medicine may place the letters "M.D." after his name, even though he is not a registered practitioner, if he do not act as such for hire or gain (g).

Where one partner was registered and the other was not, and there was painted on the sign after the name of the first "M.D., M. C. P. & S., Ont.," and after the name of the other only "M.D.," it was held that the use of the simple letters "M.D.," in contradistinction to the full titles of the partner on the same sign was not the use of a title "calculated to lead people to infer registration," and that the unregistered partner was not guilty of an offence under the act (h).

In Ontario, provision is made for the registration of Homœopathists as well as of regular practitioners, and for the Eclectics who were practising in the Province for six years before 1874.

A physician practising in another country, and performing medical services for a patient then residing there, may recover his fees in this Province notwithstanding he is not

(g) *Reg.* v. *Hessel,* 44 Ont. Q. B. 53  *Reg.* v. *Campbell,* Q. B. D. (Ont.) June, 1883.

(h) *Reg* v. *Tefft,* 45 Ont. Q. B. 144.

registered (*i*). A medical practitioner duly registered in England, under the Imperial Act, is entitled in Ontario to registration upon payment of fees without examination (*j*).

In the United States, the common law doctrine, which favours the right of every man to practise in any profession or business in which he is competent, prevails to a great extent; and medicine being regarded by it as an honorific profession, no apprenticeship was required, but the practitioner always prescribed at his peril. This was also the doctrine of the civil law, which drew no barriers around either law or medicine. Any one who pleased might practise them without any previous qualification; subject always to responsibility for injury inflicted upon others.

In the absence of any statutes, therefore, limiting the common law right to practise medicine inherent in every person, the term physician may there be applied to any one who publicly announces himself to be a practitioner of the art and undertakes to treat the sick, either for or without reward. The common law knows nothing of systems or schools of medicine. In its eyes, Eclectic, Botanic, Physio-Medical, Electrical, Thompsonian, Homœopath, Reformed, Indian Doctor, Cancer Doctor, Indianopathist, Clairvoyant Doctor and regular physician are alike. The scales of justice are no more affected by the large doses of the allopathist than by the infinitesimal supplies of the homœopathist. But the law will sometimes interfere where one not pretending to be a practising physician uses a peculiar system in his own family. A father, during the sickness of his children and wife, refused to provide any medical treatment, except that applied by himself, called the Baunscheidt system, which consists in pricking the skin of the patient in different parts of the body with an instrument armed with

---

(*i*) *Wilmot* v. *Shaw*, 2 C. L. Times, 96.
(*j*) *Reg.* v. *Coll. P. & S.* 16 C. L. J. 30; R. S. O. cap. 142, sec. 23.

a number of needles and operated by a spring, and then rubbing the parts affected with an irritating oil. The wife and three children had died within a month. The man practised the exanthematic treatment upon them, but did not even call in physicians who used that mode. The Superior Court of Pennsylvania deprived this believer in the Baunscheidt panacea of the custody of his surviving children (*k*).

Before the common law every one undertaking to treat the sick professionally, and as the exercise of his vocation, is legally a physician. He has the rights of one, and when he assumes those rights the law lays upon him the heavy burdens and responsibilities of the profession. It is, of course, far otherwise if any statute prescribes particular qualifications for the practice of the profession and one undertakes to discharge its duties without such qualifications. Then he is doubly a wrong-doer; first, as against the statute; and, second, as against the public, who have a right to demand in him the ordinary proficiency of his profession (*l*).

In Arkansas, California, Connecticut, Kentucky, Maryland, Massachusetts, Michigan, Mississippi, Missouri, New Jersey, Texas and Vermont, there appear to be no statutory requirements regulating the practice of physicians or surgeons. In Virginia, the practitioner only needs a license. In Alabama, Florida, Georgia, Louisiana, Maine, Minnesota, Ohio and Wisconsin, a practitioner must either have a license from a medical board or society, constituted according to the law of the respective States, or else be a graduate of a medical college. In South Carolina and the District of Columbia, he must be licensed by the medical board; so, too, in Delaware. But this rule in Delaware does not apply to those who practise exclusively the Thomp-

---

(*k*) *Re Heinemann's Appeal*, 96 Pa. St. 112.
(*l*) Ordronaux's Inst. of Med., secs. 5 and 6; *Sutton* v. *Tracy*, 1 Mich. 243.

sonian or botanic, or homœopathic systems; or practise gratuitously or for what is willingly given them.

In New York State, early in the century, it was enacted that no one practising physic or surgery, without a license, could collect any debts incurred by such practice, and it was a penal offence so to practise. In 1830, the unauthorized practice of physic or surgery was made a misdemeanor punishable by fine or imprisonment, or both. Shortly afterwards the offence was made penal instead of criminal, and it was declared the provisions should not extend to any one using or applying for the benefit of any sick person any roots, barks, or herbs, the growth or produce of the United States. In 1844, all laws limiting the right to practise medicine or surgery were repealed; free trade in physic prevailed; all examinations, certificates and licenses were declared unnecessary; the repealing Act expressly permitted any person to practise physic subject to punishment, as for a misdemeanor, if he should be convicted of gross ignorance, malpractice, or immoral conduct. However, a change came, and, in 1874, the legislature declared that it was "a misdemeanor for any person to practise medicine or surgery in the State of New York, unless authorized so to do by a license or diploma from some chartered school, State board of medical examiners, or medical society," or to practise under cover of a medical diploma illegally obtained. The penalty for the first offence is a fine of not more than $200; for a subsequent offence a fine of from $100 to $500, or imprisonment for not less than thirty days, or both (*m*). In 1880, it was further enacted that no person shall "practise physic or surgery within the State unless he is twenty-one years of age, and has been heretofore authorized so to do pursuant to the laws in force at the time of his authorization, or is hereafter authorized so to do, either by license from the regents of the University of the State

(*m*) N. Y. Laws, cap. 436.

of New York, a diploma of an incorporated medical college within the State, or of one without the State approved of by some proper medical faculty within the State." Every physician or surgeon, except those who had been practising ten years before 1880 (and a few others), had to register with the clerk of the county, where he practised, his name, residence, place of birth, together with his authority to practise.

After the repeal of the old Medical Acts, and before the enactment of the law of 1874, the New York Court of Common Pleas had to define who was a physician or doctor, and it said the words simply meant, " a person who made it his business to practise physic ; and it was wholly immaterial to what school of medicine he belonged, or whether he belonged to any. The legal signification of the term doctor means simply a practitioner of physic. The system pursued is immaterial. The law has nothing to do with the merits of particular systems." The point came up in considering a case where an agreement of employment between an opera director and a vocalist provided for the forfeiture of a month's salary in case the latter should fail to attend at any stated performance, except in the case of sickness, certified to by a doctor to be appointed by the director. The director appointed Dr. Quin, an homœopathist. Signor Corsi, the baritone, had a bad cold and a sore throat, but would not consult Dr. Quin, and proffered a certificate of an allopathist of his own choosing. This Max Maretzek would not take, and he refused to pay Corsi his salary. The singer sued, but the Court held that the provision was binding upon the artist, although the director had appointed a person in the practice of what is known as the homœopathic system of medicine. * * * The Court considered it was error to attempt in the then present state of medical science to recognize as a matter of law any one system of practice, or to declare that the practitioner who follows a particular system is a doctor, and that one who pursues a different method is not (*n*).

It has been held, however, that where a "regular physician" is spoken of, an allopathic is meant (*o*).

In Iowa, the Court said, "As yet there is no particular system of medicine established or favoured by the laws of Iowa, and as no system is upheld none is prohibited. The regular, the botanic, the homœopathic, the hydropathic and other modes are alike unprohibited. Though the regular system has been advancing as a science for centuries, aided by research and experiment, by experience and skill, still the law regards it with no partiality or distinguishing favour, nor is it recognized as the exclusive standard or test by which the other systems are to be adjudged" (*p*).

Notwithstanding the New York law of 1874, one can undertake to effect cures by manipulation without possessing a diploma. He may even maintain an action for the compensation agreed upon, although not a graduate and having no license to practise. A man professed to cure by rubbing, kneading and pressing the body. The court considered his system was rather one of nursing than of either medicine or surgery, and that it could not result in any injury to the person practised upon than that of possible financial loss (*q*). Yet, in Maine, where a license is required, even a "medical clairvoyant" was held to come within the statute, and it was decided that he could not render his professional services without having the legal permission. In England, an unregistered person sued to recover his charges for galvanic operations, and for materials and electric fluid used therein. The jury decided in favour of the galvanizer, and the court

---

(*n*) *Corsi* v. *Maretzek*, 4 E. D. Smith, 1.
(*o*) *Bradbury* v. *Bardin*, 35 Conn. 577.
(*p*) *Bowman* v. *Woods*, 1 Iowa, 441.
(*q*) *Smith* v. *Lane*, 24 Hun, 632.

would not disturb the verdict, as the work was done before the Act of 1858 came into operation, but expressed a strong opinion that if the work had not been done when it was, it would have been impossible to hold that the case did not fall within the statute (*r*).

A physician must practise according to the principles of his school. There are distinct and different schools of practice; allopathic or old school, homœopathic, Thompsonian, hydropathic or water cure; and if a physician of one of those schools is called in, his treatment is to be tested by the general doctrines of his school, not by those of other schools. It is presumed that patient and physician both understand this (*s*).

A person professing to follow one system of medical treatment cannot be expected by his employer to practise another. While the regular physician is expected to follow the rules of the old school in the art of curing, the botanic physician must be equally expected to adhere to his adopted method. While on the part of every medical practitioner the law implies an undertaking that he will use an ordinary degree of care and skill in medical operations, and he is unquestionably liable for gross carelessness or unskilfulness in the management of his patients, still the person who employs a botanic practitioner has no right to expect the same kind of treatment or the same kind of medicine that a regular physician would administer. The law does not require a man to accomplish more than he undertakes, nor in a different manner from what he professes. So, if one is employed as a botanic physician, and performs his services with ordinary care and skill, in accordance with the system he professes to follow, that will be regarded as a legal defence to a suit for malpractice. It would show a full com-

---

(*r*) *Bibber* v. *Simpson*, 59 Me. 181; *Thistleton* v. *Frewer*, 31 L. J. Ex. 230.

(*s*) *Patten* v. *Wiggin*, 51 Me. 594.

pliance with his profession and undertaking, and if injury resulted to the plaintiff he could blame no one but himself (t).

If a patient has not been deluded by any but himself, and voluntarily employs in one art a man who openly exercises another, his folly has no claim to indulgence. The old Mahomedan case, cited by Puffendorf with approbation, is very much to the point. A man who had a disorder in his eyes called on a farrier for a remedy. This worthy gave him a remedy commonly used by his quadrupedal patients. The man lost his sight, and brought an action against the farrier for damages; but the Judge said that no action would lie, for, if the complainant had not himself been an ass, he would never have employed a horse doctor. But when a case, the converse of this, came up, the Court remarked that, "stock and the human family are animals with many similitudes and some variances; so that, although it be admitted that one acquainted with the mode of treating diseases of the human family should not be relied on to select from the materia medica substances apt for the treatment of stock, still we think it clear that one having a scientific knowledge of the diseases of men must be presumed to have so much knowledge of the diseases of a mule as to enable him to determine whether a disease with which the animal is afflicted be of recent or long standing. An expert in the diseases of man is necessarily an expert in the diseases of animals, so as to make his opinion competent evidence upon a matter in reference to which he will swear that his scientific knowledge has enabled him to form an opinion." And so a physician was allowed to give his opinion as to whether the disease with which a mule was afflicted was, or was not, of long standing, as he considered himself competent so to do from his knowledge

---

(t) *Bowman* v. *Woods*, 1 Iowa, 441.

of the diseases to which human flesh is heir, although he knew nothing in particular about the diseases of stock (*u*).

As one who employs a homœopathic or botanic physician knowingly cannot object to his bill because he was not treated in the way usual among orthodox practitioners; so, on the other hand, if a physician of one school is employed by one who has a *penchant* for that particular system, and treats his patient according to a different system, he cannot recover for his services if he fail to benefit the patient (*v*).

Proof that one practises physic is *prima facie* evidence of his professional character; and if one holds himself out as a physician and surgeon, and acts as such, the law will hold him liable as such (*w*).

A physician who merely casually makes up a prescription for a friend when meeting him upon the street, cannot be called his medical attendant; that term means one to whose care a sick person has been confided (*x*).

(*u*) *Horton* v. *Green*, 64 N. C. 64.
(*v*) Ordronaux, sec. 8.
(*w*) *Sutton* v. *Tracy*, 1 Mich. 243; *Reynolds* v. *Graves*, 3 Wisc. 416.
(*x*) *Langdon* v. *Mut. Life Ins. Co.*, 5 Hun. N. Y. 1.

## CHAPTER V.

### NEGLIGENCE AND MALPRACTICE.

Malpractice, or *mala praxis*, may be defined to be an improper discharge of professional duties, either through want of skill or negligence. It is now more particularly applied to torts—when committed by a physician, surgeon, or apothecary.

It is a great misdemeanour and offence at common law, whether it arise from curiosity and experiment, or from neglect; because it breaks the trust which the party has placed in the physician, tending directly to his destruction (a). A medical man who is guilty of gross negligence, or evinces a gross ignorance of his profession, is criminally responsible for the consequences. And one who, by a culpable want of care and attention, or by the absence of a competent degree of skill and knowledge, causes injury to a patient, is liable to a civil action for damages; unless, indeed, such injury be the immediate result of intervening negligence on the part of the patient himself; or unless such patient has by his own carelessness directly conduced to such injury (b).

It is sometimes difficult to distinguish between civil and criminal malpractice, or to say when one is criminally, and when only civilly responsible. But it may be said generally, that to constitute criminal liability there must be such a

---

(a) Per Cur., in *Dr. Greonvelt's* case, 1 Lord Ray, 213.
(b) Glenn, p. 251; Addison on Torts, Ed. 3rd, p. 17.

degree of complete negligence in the practice as the law means by the word felonious (c).

There may be malpractice by commission, *i. e.*, from the want of ordinary skill in the discharge of professional duties; or malpractice by omission, *i. e.*, from negligence in the discharge of such duties.

The question, " Was there negligence?" will be answered from the stand point of the law, not from that of medicine, when a matter comes to be judicially investigated. The law as applicable to other professions and occupations will be applied to the medical or surgical case under consideration.

Strictly speaking, the term *negligence* is limited in its application to carelessness in the performance of professional duty; *carelessness* is its proper synonyme. Duties performed without care, caution, attention, diligence, skill, prudence, or judgment, are negligently performed. Acts are so designated which are performed by one heedlessly, even when there is no purpose to omit the performance of duty. It is *non-feasance*, not malfeasance. It is the omitting to do, and not the ill-doing—it is the leaving undone what one ought to have done—not the doing what one ought not to have done—this last being a want of skill. In its various degrees it ranges between simple accident and actual fraud, the latter beginning where negligence ends (d).

Wharton, after criticising various definitions, proposes this, " Negligence, in its civil relations, is such an inadvertent imperfection, by a responsible human agent, in the discharge of a legal duty, as immediately produces, in an ordinary and natural sequence, a damage to another" (e). Negli-

---
(c) Glenn, p. 252; Erle, C.J., *R.* v. *Noakes*, 4 F. & F. 920.
(d) *Gardiner* v. *Heartt*, 3 Denio, 232-236; McClelland's Civil Malpractice, cap. 17.
(e) Wharton on Negligence, sec. 3.

gence, in medical practice, is a violation of the obligation that medical men impliedly enter into when they accept the charge of a patient; such obligation enjoins care and caution in what they do, and in what they omit to do. A medical man is liable as well for want of skill, as for negligence, and an injured party may bring his action to recover for damage resulting from ignorance and carelessness, and recover on proving that he sustained damage from either (*f*).

Physicians and surgeons have specified duties imposed upon them when they undertake the charge of a patient. Refusing to perform their part of the implied contract will constitute negligence, and for all injury resulting therefrom they will be held accountable. It will constitute a tort for which the law gives damages (*g*). Of course a medical man, unless he be an officer of the Government, charged with specific duties which he thereby violates, has a legal right to decline to take charge of a particular case. When in charge, however, he is liable for any negligence, whether of omission or commission, which may produce injury to his patient. *Voluntatis est suscipere mandatum, necessitas est consummare* (*h*).

There is an implied obligation on a man holding himself out to the community as a physician and surgeon, and practising his profession, that he should possess the ordinary skill requisite for reasonable success, and that he should attend to the case with due care (*i*). If the patient knows of the practitioner's want of skill, he cannot complain of the lack of that which he knew did not exist.

(*f*) *Carpenter* v. *Blake*, 60 Barb. 488.
(*g*) McClelland, cap. 17.
(*h*) Wharton, sec. 731.
(*i*) *Wilmot* v. *Howard*, 32 Vt. 447; *Long* v. *Morrison*, 14 Ind. 595; *Patten* v. *Wiggin*, 51 Me. 594.

A surgeon does not become an actual insurer (*j*); the implied contract is not to cure, but to possess and employ in the treatment of the case such reasonable skill and diligence as are ordinarily exercised by thoroughly educated surgeons; and in judging of the degree of skill and attention required, regard is to be had to the time and place. The law implies that in the treatment of all cases which they undertake medical men will exercise reasonable and ordinary care and diligence; they are bound always to use their best skill and judgment in determining the nature of the malady and the best mode of treatment, and in all respects to do their best to secure a perfect restoration of their patients to health and soundness. But they do not impliedly warrant the recovery of their patients, and are not liable on account of any failure in that respect, unless it is through some default of their own (*k*). Tindal, C.J., in summing up to the jury in an action for improper treatment to a hand and wrist, whereby the plaintiff lost the use of her hand, well said, "Every person who enters into a learned profession undertakes to bring to the exercise of it a reasonable degree of care and skill. He does not undertake, if he is a surgeon, that he will perform a cure, nor does he undertake to use the highest possible degree of skill. There may be persons who have higher education and greater advantages than he has, but he undertakes to bring a fair, reasonable and competent degree of skill."

Wharton and Stillé thus state the law: "A physician and surgeon is only responsible for ordinary skill, etc., and for the exercise of his best judgment in matters of doubt. He is not accountable for a want of the highest degree of skill (*l*), nor for an erroneous, though honest conclusion,

---

(*j*) *Hancke* v. *Hooper*, 7 C. & P. 81.

(*k*) *Patten* v. *Wiggin*, 51 Me. 594.

(*l*) *Leighton* v. *Sargent*, 7 Fost. 460; *Simonds* v. *Henry*, 39 Me. 155; *Hancke* v. *Hooper*, 7 C. & P. 81; *McCandless* v. *McWha*, 22 Pa. St. 261; *Carpenter* v. *Blake*, 60 Barb. 488; *Utley* v. *Burns*, 70 Ill. 162; *Barnes* v. *Means*, 82 Ill. 379.

according to his best light (*m*). The law has no allowance for quackery. It demands qualification in the profession practised, not extraordinary skill such as belongs to few men of rare genius and endowment, but that degree which ordinarily characterizes the profession. And in determining whether the practitioner possesses ordinary skill, regard must be had to the advanced state of the profession at the time *(n)*.

As to what is ordinary or reasonable skill or care, the rule has sometimes been laid down thus favourably, "The least amount of skill with which a fair proportion of the practitioners of a given locality are endowed, is to be taken as the criterion by which to judge the physician's skill or ability" (*o*). Or, as another writer puts it, "It has been finally determined to consider the least amount of skill compatible with a scientific knowledge of the healing art as sufficient to predicate the existence of ordinary skill" (*p*). To render a medical man liable even civilly for negligence, or want of due care or skill, it is not enough that there has been a less degree of skill than some other medical man may have shown, or a less degree of care than even he himself might have bestowed, nor is it enough that he himself acknowledges some degree of want of care; there must have been a want of competent and ordinary care and skill, and to such a degree as to have led to a bad result (*q*).

In a city there are many means of professional culture which are inaccessible in the country. Hospitals can be walked, libraries visited, new books and appliances bought,

(*m*) *Heath* v. *Gibson*, 3 Oregon, 64.
(*n*) *Slater* v. *Baker*, 2 Wils. 359; *McCandless* v. *McWha*, sup.; Wh. and Still. Medic. Juris. sec. 1087.
(*o*) Bouvier's Institutes, secs. 1004-1005.
(*p*) Ordronaux's Jurisp. of Medicine, sec. 23.
(*q*) *Rich* v. *Pierpoint*, 3 F. & F. 35.

constant intercourse had with the greater lights of the profession. What is due diligence, therefore, in the city, is not due diligence in the country; and what is due diligence in the country is not due diligence in the city. Hence, the question, in each particular case, is to be determined, not by enquiring what would be the average diligence or skill of the profession (which would be a thing very difficult to reach), but what would be the diligence or skill of an honest, intelligent and responsible practitioner in the position in which the one in question was placed (*r*).

The skill required is not an *absolute* but a *relative* qualification; and as such, therefore, always subordinated to whatever conventional standard of professional proficiency we may choose to adopt. Like morals, it may vary with times and places, or, if based upon representative intellects, it is clear that the ideal type selected must be one to which the majority, rather than the minority, of minds approximate (*s*). A physician, when called upon to manage a case, is not required to apply the skill and care which could be applied by the perfect ideal physician, for the reason that from the limitation of the human intellect no perfect ideal physician exists in practice, and, from the limitation of human endurance, no perfect ideal physician, even if he existed, could watch a patient unintermittingly. But a physician, when called upon to manage a case, is bound to exercise the skill and vigilance which good and faithful physicians, under the circumstances in which he is placed, would exercise. If called upon in a country town, remote from the great centres of scientific activity, to attend to an exceptional case which requires immediate action, he is not liable if he does not employ those mechanisms which only a residence in such a centre of scientific activity would enable him to procure. On the other hand, a physician living in such a

(*r*) Wharton on Negligence, sec. 734.
(*s*) Ordronaux, sec. 22.

centre is liable for negligence, if, when called upon in such a case, he does not use such mechanism, supposing its application to be advisable (*t*).

A physician and surgeon is bound to possess the ordinary skill, learning and experience of his profession generally at the time in similar localities, and with similar opportunities for experience (*u*).

A patient is entitled to the benefit of the increased knowledge of the day. The physician or surgeon who assumes to exercise the healing art is bound to be up to the improvements of the day. The standard of ordinary skill is on the advance; and he who would not be found wanting must apply himself with all diligence to the most accredited sources of knowledge (*v*).

Sex is no excuse for negligence; there is no rule of law to the effect that less care is required of a woman than a man. A lady physician cannot as such claim any privilege of exemption from the care and caution required of men, any more than a woman acting as a locomotive engineer could be allowed to use less diligence to avoid mischief to others than men must use. Male and female are governed by the same rule in this respect: the rule of prudent regard for the rights of others knows nothing of sex (*w*). Inasmuch as gratuitous services are more generally rendered by young and inexperienced physicians than by those who are well established in their business, a presumption naturally arises that one who renders such services is not possessed of great skill, and was not supposed to be by the patient. This presumption may be overcome by proof to the contrary; and the physician must be judged by the

---

(*t*) Wharton on Negligence, sec. 640.

(*u*) *Small* v. *Howard*, 128 Mass. 131; *Hathorn* v. *Richmond*, 48 Vt. 557.

(*v*) Woodward, J., in *McCandless* v. *McWha*, 22 Pa. Rep. 261.

(*w*) *Mich. Cent. Rw.* v. *Hasseneyer*, 48 Mich. 205; *Fox* v. *Glastonbury*, 29 Conn. 204.

standard to which he led the patient to believe he had attained; or, if he has done nothing to mislead his patient upon this point, his responsibility will be measured by the degree of skill which he is proved actually to possess (*x*).

It has been laid down in Maine, that physicians and surgeons who offer themselves to the public as practitioners impliedly promise thereby that they possess the requisite skill and knowledge to enable them to heal such cases as they undertake with reasonable success; and that this rule does not require the possession of the highest, or even the average skill, knowledge and experience, but only such as will enable them to treat the case understandingly and safely (*y*).

Considering how much the treatment of a case depends upon its varying phases, which change as quickly as the shifting hues of the heavens, it is hard for one medical man to come forward and condemn the treatment of a brother in the profession, and to say he would have done this or that, when probably, had he been in a position to judge of the case from the first, he would have done no better (*z*).

If a physician does not bring to the treatment of an injury or of a disease the ordinary amount of skill possessed by those in his profession, it is immaterial how high his standing may be; if he has skill and does not apply it he is guilty of negligence, and if he does not have it then he is liable for the want of it. When a case of alleged malpractice is before the court, the questions to be considered are: Did the defendant possess the ordinary skill of persons acting as medical men? If he did, was he chargeable in not applying it in the treatment of the patient? Whether

(*x*) Shearman & Red., sec. 432.
(*y*) *Patten* v. *Wiggen*, 51 Me. 594.
(*z*) *Rich* v. *Pierpoint*, per Erle, C.J., 3 F. & F. 35.

he possessed greater skill, or had been successful in the treatment of other patients, is wholly immaterial. Where the point in issue is whether skill was applied in a given case, the possession of skill without proof that it was applied will be no defence (a).

The law punishes negligence no less than want of skill. It is undoubtedly true that the physician is the best judge of the degree of attention which any case requires. Nor is it in the omission to make a given number of visits that negligence resides, but whenever any important step in the treatment of disease is neglected, or any important stage of it overlooked, which might have been used for the benefit of the patient, then it may be averred that the physician has been guilty of negligence, however assiduous he may otherwise have been at different periods of his treatment. Skill and diligence may be considered, therefore, as indissolubly associated, since skill judges of the measure of diligence required and also furnishes the latter with the eyes of observation and the hands of execution ; while diligence on her part gives cumulative power to skill, and leaves no link wanting in the continuous train of treatment (b). The measure of skill which a physician is bound to exercise is not affected by his refusal of the proffer of assistance from other medical men (c). The Court said that such a refusal is no more than an implied declaration of ability to treat the case properly. By assuming and continuing the charge of the patient, the physician is under an obligation to exercise a degree of skill which is neither increased or diminished by such refusal.

In considering the skill and knowledge of a practitioner regard must be had to the school to which he professes to

(a) *Carpenter* v. *Blake*, 60 Barb. 488.
(b) Ordronaux's Jur. of Med., sec. 68.
(c) *Potter* v. *Warner*, 91 Pa. St. 362 ; 36 Am. Rep. 668.

belong; and where there is no particular system established or favoured by law, and no system is prohibited, every physician is expected to practise according to his professed and avowed system. A botanic physician is to be gauged according to the botanic system, and a homœopathic physician by the homœopathic system: so if a botanic doctor, or a homœopathist, is sued for malpractice he may free himself from blame by showing that his practice was according to the rules of the school which he professed and was known to follow, and a departure from the received canons of his system will be taken as a want of ordinary skill. But the jury is not to judge by determining which school in their own view is best (*d*).

A sign or other proof that one actually practises physic or surgery is *prima facie* evidence of his professional character (*e*). And when a physician's skill is at issue he may adduce evidence to prove the existence of such general skill on his part, irrespective of the particular case as to which the question arises; and he may show this by the testimony of those in his profession who can speak from personal knowledge of his practice (*f*).

The possession of a medical diploma is *prima facie* of ordinary skill. But of course it must be shown that the college from which it emanated had authority to grant degrees in medicine (*g*).

If, in the absence of a medical man, a non-professional person is called in to assist a person taken suddenly sick, such amateur is not liable for special or slight negligence,

---

(*d*) *Bowman* v. *Woods*, 1 Greene (Iowa), 441; *Corsi* v. *Maretzek*, 4 E. D. Smith, 1.

(*e*) *Sutton* v. *Tracy*, 1 Mich. 243.

(*f*) *Mertz* v. *Detweiler*, 8 W. & Serg. 376; *Seare* v. *Prentice*, 8 East, 348; *Carpenter* v. *Blake*, 60 Barb. 518.

(*g*) *Hunter* v. *Blount*, 27 Ga. 76; *Leighton* v. *Sargent*, 7 Foster, N. H. 476.

that is for the lack of that diligence and skill belonging to a professed physician; but he is liable for gross negligence (the *culpa lata* of the Latinists), that is, the lack of the diligence and skill belonging to ordinary unprofessional persons of common sense; while, as we have seen, the physician is liable for slight negligence (*culpa levis*), if he either undertakes the case without the ordinary qualifications of a physician under such circumstances, or manages it without the ordinary skill of such a physician (*h*).

If a physician treats a patient without being requested so to do, he is held to a more strict account than in ordinary cases. In one instance, a medical man administered physic to a slave without the owner's consent, and the court held him responsible for all the evil consequences which resulted (*i*); and this rule is still more rigidly enforced when the volunteer by his officiousness excludes a competent practitioner who would have been otherwise obtainable. If one who is not a regular medical practitioner professes to deal with the life and health of others, he is bound to have and employ competent skill (*j*).

The mere fact that he renders his services gratuitously, or out of charity, does not free the practitioner from all liability. But, according to some authorities, the attendant in such cases is held to a less strict accountability than when his services are based upon an implied contract, and is liable only for gross negligence (*k*). Amos, in his "Science of Law," says, "The less the payment made in return for diligence, the less the diligence that is expected; and if no payment at all is made, as little diligence as possible is

---

(*h*) Wharton on Negligence, sec. 29.
(*i*) *Hood* v. *Grimes*, 13 B. Monr. 188.
(*j*) *Ruddock* v. *Lowe*, 4 F. & F. 519; *R.* v. *Simpson*, 4 C. & P. 407, note.
(*k*) Shearman & Redfield on Negligence, sec. 432; *Ritchey* v. *West*, 3 Ill. 385; *Shiells* v. *Blackburne*, 1 H. Bl. 159; *Wilson* v. *Brett*, 11 M .2 &W. 113; *Pippin* v. *Shepherd*, 11 Price, 400.

usually expected, though it may be that some is." Wharton cannot accept this doctrine from humane and other considerations (*l*). And Ordronaux says that it may be considered as a received principle of law that, a physician, though rendering his services gratuitously, as in hospitals or among the out-door poor, is bound to exibibit the same degree of ordinary skill and diligence in the treatment of a patient as if he were acting under the incentive of a consideration or prospective reward. If he undertakes to execute the trust reposed in him, he is bound to do it well, or else he may be compelled to respond in damages to the party injured by his misfeasance. It is not the consideration which constitutes the foundation of his responsibility, but the fact that in voluntarily accepting the mandate, *spondet peritiam artis*, indiscriminately to all. He cannot apportion medical skill or his diligence to meet the prospective emoluments flowing out of any given case (*m*).

In a criminal case, Denman, J., told the jury that it made no difference whether a medical man was dealing with a patient or acting as a volunteer, and dealing with a friend or with his own wife (*n*). But Cockburn, C.J., in a case where a patient in a hospital sued two surgeons for injury received from being scalded in a bath, in which he had been placed by the nurses on the orders of the surgeons, said, no doubt persons who went as patients into hospitals were not to be treated with negligence; but, on the other hand, medical gentlemen who gave their services gratuitously were not to be made liable for negligence for which they were not personally responsible. The jury gave a verdict in favour of the doctors (*o*).

If a sick man applies to one, not a physician, for gratui-

(*l*) Wharton on Negligence, sec. 731 n.
(*m*) Jur. of Med. sec. 27.
(*n*) *R. v. Macleod*, 12 Cox. C. C. 534.
(*o*) *Perionowsky v. Freeman*, 4 F. & F. 977.

tous medical assistance, and this one either does not exert all his skill, or administers improper medicine to the best of his ability, he is not liable for damage (*p*).

The amount of prudence which a man must exercise in selecting a physician, and the means to be cured, is the same that any prudent and reasonable man would do in any other matter (*q*).

It is the duty of a patient to co-operate with his medical adviser, and to conform to the necessary prescriptions; and if, under the pressure of pain, he does not, or, if by refusing to adopt the remedies of the physician, he frustrates the latter's endeavours, or, if he aggravates the case by his own misconduct, he cannot charge against the physician the consequences due distinctively to himself; for no one can take advantage of his own wrong. In such a case, even if the physician's treatment was objectionable, he can only recover nominal damages; and if the injury was due to the patient's fractiousness and disregard of the doctor's orders (the latter being judicious), no action at all will lie (*r*).

In Ohio, it was held that, in an action for malpractice in the treatment of a swollen ankle and diseased foot, the Judge had not erred in saying to the jury, "If you find that the defendant directed the plaintiff to observe absolute rest as a part of the treatment to his foot, and that direction was such as a surgeon or physician of ordinary skill would adopt or sanction, and the patient negligently failed to observe such direction, or purposely disobeyed the same, and that such negligence or disobedience approximately

---

(*p*) *Shiells* v. *Blackburne*, 1 H. Bl. 159.

(*q*) *Boynton* v. *Somersworth*, 58 N. H. 321.

(*r*) McClelland, Civil Malpractice; Wharton on Negligence, sec. 737; *Leighton* v. *Sargent*, 7 Fost. 460; *McCandless* v. *McWha*, 22 Pa. St. 261.

contributed to the injury of which he complains, he cannot recover in this action; although he may prove that the defendant's negligence and want of skill also contributed to the injury. The injured party must not have contributed at all." The information given by a surgeon to his patient concerning the nature of his malady is a circumstance that should be considered in determining whether the patient, in disobeying the instructions of the surgeon, was guilty of negligence or not (*s*).

The general doctrine of contributory negligence is this, that although there may have been negligence on the part of the plaintiff, yet, unless he might, by the exercise of ordinary care, have avoided the consequence of the defendant's negligence, he is entitled to recover; if, by ordinary care, he might have avoided it, then he is the author of his own wrong (*t*). The rule is laid down in another case as follows: If it be impossible to separate the injury occasioned by the plaintiff from that occasioned by the neglect of the defendant, the plaintiff cannot recover; if, however, they can be separated, for such injury as the plaintiff may show thus preceded solely from the want of ordinary skill or ordinary care of the defendant, he may recover (*u*).

The patient must exercise ordinary care and prudence; he is not bound to observe the utmost possible caution. And the ordinary care required has been defined to be that degree of care which persons of ordinary care and prudence are accustomed to use and employ under similar circumstances (*v*). In fact the plaintiff must use his own senses (*w*). Still, if he is rash and negligent, and yet the

(*s*) *Geiselman* v. *Scott*, 25 Oh. St. 86.
(*t*) *Parker* v. *Adams*, 12 Metc. 417.
(*u*) *Hibbard* v. *Thompson*, 109 Mass 286.
(*v*) *Cleveland, etc., Rw.* v. *Terry*, 8 Oh. St. 570.
(*w*) *Ch. & R. I. Rw.* v. *McKean*, 40 Ill. 218; *Eakin* v. *Brown*, 1 E. D. Smith, 36.

physician has been so very neglectful that ordinary care on the part of the patient would not have prevented the unfortunate result, the plaintiff will be entitled to recover damages (*x*). So, where the doctor's negligence is the proximate cause of the injury, and that of the patient only the remote cause (*y*). And proximate does not mean the first or nearest in order of time, but the first or nearest in order of cause (*z*).

It is to be remembered that a physician may be called to prescribe for cases which originated in the carelessness of the patient; and though such carelessness would remotely contribute to the injury sued for, it would not relieve the physician from liability for his distinct negligence and the separate injury occasioned thereby. The patient may also, while he is under treatment, injure himself by his own carelessness; yet he may recover of the physician, if he carelessly or unskilfully treats him afterwards, and thus does him a distinct injury (*a*). The burden of proving that the plaintiff's own negligence contributed to the injury rests upon the defendant (*b*). Evidence that the patient requested the defendant to perform an operation, or do an act, which caused the injury, does not tend to prove contributory negligence, if the injury was not the natural result of such act carefully performed (*c*).

If the patient is insane, and so incapable of co-operating with the physician, contributory negligence is not imputable. And this inability the physician is bound to take into account (*d*).

(*x*) *Clark* v. *Kerwin*, 4 E. D. Smith, 21; *Parker* v. *Adams*, 12 Mete 417.
(*y*) *Kerwhaker* v. *Cleveland, etc., Rw.* 3 Oh. 172; *Ind. and Cin. Rw.* v. *Caldwell*, 9 Ind. 397.
(*z*) *Ch. etc., Rw.* v. *Goss*, 17 Wisc. 428.
(*a*) Chapman, C.J., *Hibbard* v. *Thompson*, 109 Mass. 288.
(*b*) *Gramm* v. *Boener*, 56 Ind. 497.
(*c*) *Fisk* v. *Wait*, 104 Mass. 71.
(*d*) *People* v. *N. Y. Hospital*, 3 Abb. N. C. 229.

If the physician has injured the patient by his negligence, the refusal of the patient, or his custodian, to allow an experiment, by another physician, to repair the injury is not contributory negligence, unless he had reasonable assurance of the success of the experiment (*e*).

The practitioner is liable where a patient suffers from his want of ordinary skill and diligence, even though the carelessness of those nursing the patient may have aggravated the case and rendered the ultimate condition of the patient worse than it otherwise would have been. Although this carelessness in nursing may be proved in mitigation of the damages sought against the physician, it will not serve to bar the right of action (*f*). And where two surgeons, who gave their services gratuitously to the sick in a hospital, were sued by one Perionowsky, for maltreatment there by causing him to be placed in a bath so hot that he was scalded and injured, and it was proved that the bath, though ordered by the defendants, was actually administered by the nurses, and that the defendants were not present when it was given, and that it was no part of their duty personally to superintend such things. Cockburn, C.J., in summing up, told the jury that the surgeons would not be liable for the neglect of the nurses unless near enough to be aware of it and to prevent it (*g*). And, in another case, the court held that if a jury were to find that the parents of the patient (a boy) were in charge of and nursed him during his sickness, and that they did not obey the directions of the physician in regard to the treatment and care of their son during such time, but disregarded the same, and thereby contributed to the several injuries of which he complains, he could not recover. If the injuries were

---

(*e*) *Chamberland* v. *Morgan*, 68 Penn. St. 168.

(*f*) *Wilmot* v. *Howard*, 39 Vt. 447.

(*g*) *Perionowsky* v. *Freeman*, 4 F. & F. 977.

the result of mutual and concurring neglect of the parties no action to recover damages therefor will lie (*h*).

The medical man has ofttimes to sail between Scylla and Charybdis. While, on the one hand, he is bound to consult the attainable literature in his profession, and to diligently gather in, for every case he undertakes to treat, the experience of his confreres—for in determining what is negligence, the improvements that are constantly taking place are always considered—at the same time he must not try new modes or methods too readily, lest a Judge say of him, as one said in a surgery case, "It appears from the evidence of the surgeons that it was improper to disunite the callus without consent. This is the usage and law of surgeons. Then it was ignorance and unskilfulness, in that very particular, to do contrary to the rule of the profession what no surgeon ought to have done. For anything that appears to the court, this was the first experiment made with this new instrument; and, if it was, it was a rash action, and he who acts rashly acts ignorantly; and although the defendants (a surgeon and an apothecary), in general, may be as skilful in their respective professions as any two gentlemen in England, yet the court cannot help saying that, in this particular case, they acted ignorantly and unskilfully, contrary to the known rule and usage of surgeons;" (and they had to pay the plaintiff £500 for the damage to his leg) (*i*). Success is the only thing that justifies an innovation either in politics or physic.

When it is proved that the physician has omitted altogether the established mode of treatment, and has adopted one that has proved to be injurious, evidence of skill, or of reputation for skill, is wholly immaterial, except to show (what the law presumes) that he possesses the ordinary

(*h*) *Potter* v. *Warner*, 91 Penn. St. 362.
(*i*) *Slater* v. *Baker*, 2 Wils. 359.

degree of skill of persons engaged in the same profession. In such a case, it is of no consequence how much skill he may have; he has demonstrated a want of it in the treatment of the particular case.

The failure to use skill, if the surgeon has it, may be negligence; but when the treatment adopted is not in accordance with the established practice, but is positively injurious, the case is not one of negligence, but of want of skill. If the case is a new one, the patient must trust to the skill and experience of the surgeon he calls. So must he if the injury or disease is attended with injury to other parts, or other diseases have developed themselves, for which there is no established mode of treatment. But when the case is one as to which a system of treatment has been followed for a long time, there should be no departure from it, unless the surgeon who does it is prepared to take the risk of establishing by his success the propriety and safety of his experiment. This rule protects the community against reckless experiments, while it admits the adoption of new remedies and modes of treatment only when their benefits have been demonstrated, or where, from the necessity of the case, the surgeon or physician must be left to the exercise of his own skill and experience (*j*).

Physicians are not bound to comply with the demands of the public; they may accept or refuse a call: but having accepted, one must continue in attendance upon the case until recovery, unless dismissed, or unless he has withdrawn in a proper way. Even if his services are gratuitous, he must continue them until reasonable time has been given to procure other attendance.

A husband sued a medical man for neglecting to attend

---

(*j*) *Carpenter* v. *Blake*, 60 Barb. 488.

his wife, according to agreement, during childbirth, and the jury gave him a verdict of $500; the court considered that the physician had broken his contract and was liable therefor, but reduced the damages to a nominal sum, as, in an action on contract, the husband could not recover for the personal injury and sufferings of the wife (*k*).

If a physician at any time desires to withdraw from a case, he must give such reasonable notice as will enable the patient to obtain assistance elsewhere. He has a right to withdraw at any time, especially with his patient's consent, but if he insists upon that assent as a shield from liability for any negligence of which he may have been guilty, or for any malpractice committed, the patient may show, if he can, that the consent was obtained by representations that were false; and then the consent will be no protection against liability for damage that had occurred before the consent was given (*l*).

While it is quite competent for a physician and his patient to make any agreement they think fit, limiting the attendance to a longer or shorter period, or to a single visit; and while, if there is no such limitation, the physician can discontinue his attendance at his own pleasure, after giving reasonable notice of his intention to do so; yet, if he is sent for at the time of an injury by one whose family physician he has been for years, the effect of his responding to the call will be an engagement to attend upon the case so long as it requires attention, unless he gives notice to the contrary, or is discharged by the patient; and he is bound to use ordinary care and skill, not only in his attendance but in determining when it may be safely and properly discontinued (*m*). Ordronaux says a physician cannot

---

(*k*) *Hunter* v. *Ogden*, 31 U. C. R. 132.
(*l*) *Carpenter* v. *Blake*, Sup.
(*m*) *Ballou* v. *Prescott*, 64 Me. 305.

abandon a case without due notice. To do so would constitute negligence of a grave character, and render him answerable for all injury sustained by the patient in consequence thereof. The contract is for the performance of a service of indefinite duration, and usually without stipulation for its continuance during any particular period. It is plainly a fraud upon the employer to abandon or neglect discharging the trust after having accepted it, for the acceptance constitutes a promise, and a promise is a good foundation upon which to rest a legal obligation. If the physician retires from it, he can only do so by placing the employer in as good circumstances as he found him, and by giving due notice of his intention (*n*).

A medical man is liable to a civil action for injury resulting to a patient from his negligence or unskilful treatment, although the patient neither employed nor was to pay him. As Baron Parke said: "If an apothecary administers improper medicines to his patient, or a surgeon unskilfully treats him, and thereby injures his health, he will be liable to the patient, even where the father or friend of the patient may have been the contracting party with the apothecary or surgeon; for, though no such contract had been made, the apothecary, if he gave improper medicines, or the surgeon, if he took him as a patient and unskilfully treated him, would be liable to an action for a misfeasance (*o*). And as Richards, C.B., said: "From the necessity of the thing, the only person who can properly sustain an action for damages for an injury done to the person of a patient, is the patient himself, for damages could not be given on that account to any other person, although the surgeon may have been retained and employed by him to undertake the case"(*p*); and in this same case, which was an

(*n*) Ordronaux, sec. 14 ; Shearman & Red., sec. 441.
(*o*) *Longmeid* v. *Holliday*, 6 Ex. 767.
(*p*) *Pippin* v. *Sheppard*, 11 Price, 400.

action brought by a husband and a wife for an injury done to the wife, Garrow, B., said; "In the practice of surgery, the public are exposed to great risks from the number of ignorant persons professing a knowledge of the art, without the least pretensions to the most necessary qualifications, and they often inflict very serious injury on those who are so unfortunate as to fall into their hands. In cases of the most brutal inattention and neglect, the patients would be precluded frequently from seeking damages by course of law, if it were necessary to enable them to recover, that there should have been a previous retainer, on their part, of the person professing to be able to cure them. In all cases of surgeons retained by any public establishments, it would happen that the patient would be without redress, for it could hardly be expected that the governors of an infirmary should bring an action against the surgeon employed by them to attend the child of poor parents, who may have suffered from his negligence and inattention"(q).

As in the case of an attorney, so with a physician, it is not every mistake or misapprehension that will make him liable to an action for negligence. There is scarcely a case in which a physician is called in, in which he may not be charged with *culpa levissima*, or the omission to ward off every possible casualty; and if *culpa levissima* makes him liable, then his liability becomes almost co-extensive with his practice. He is only responsible for *culpa levis* (r).

It must be remembered that the implied liability of a physician or surgeon, retained to treat a case professionally, extends no further, in the absence of a special agreement, than that he will indemnify his patient against any injurious consequences resulting from his want of the proper degree of skill, care or diligence, in the execution of his

---

(q) *Gladwell* v. *Steggall*, 5 Bing. N. C. 733.
(r) Wharton on Negligence, sec. 735.

employment; and in an action against the surgeon for malpractice, the plaintiff, if he shows no injury resulting from negligence or want of skill in the defendant, will not be entitled to recover even nominal damages (s).

The question whether the physician possessed adequate skill, and exercised adequate care, is, in a case of malpractice, for the jury to decide. Theoretically, and we may add, literally, the jury have the unquestioned right to decide every controverted fact, even if its decision may involve the most abstrusively difficult and uncertain questions in the regions of scientific enquiry. But it is for the Judge to determine whether there is or not such evidence as ought reasonably to satisfy the jury that the fact sought to be proved is established. As Lord Cairns once put it, "The Judge has to say whether any facts have been established by evidence from which negligence *may be reasonably inferred*, the jury have to say whether from these facts, when submitted to them, *negligence ought to be inferred*." It is for the Judge to say whether the case should or should not be submitted to the jury; and the rule is imperative that it should not be, unless the evidence be such that therefrom the negligence charged may be reasonably inferred (t).

Judges are generally desirous of impressing on juries the necessity of construing everything in the most favourable way for the defendant, when such actions are brought against a surgeon. "It is notorious there are many cases in which jurors are not the most dispassionate or most competent persons to try the rights of parties, and an action of this kind (*i. e.*, against a surgeon for malpractice) comes within this class. In such actions the Judge should

---

(s) *Craig* v. *Chambers*, 17 Ohio St. 253.
(t) *Fields* v. *Rutherford*, 29 (Ont.) C. P. 113; *Metropolitan R. W. Co.* v. *Jackson*, L. R. 3 App. 193, 197.

firmly assume the responsibility of determining himself whether sufficient evidence has or has not been given to compel him to leave the case to the jury" (*u*).

Medical writers speak strongly against such actions. One says, " In the majority of cases these actions are the direct offspring of envy, hatred, malice and all uncharitableness, and when, rocked in the cradle of calumny and nursed by the hand of speculation, injury is often inflicted upon the character of the physician, who is at the same time left without any proper remedy at law. The effect, also, of such suits upon the public mind is apt to be pernicious, for success in obtaining damages often stimulates others into a repetition of the experiment, and the physician consequently practises his art in chains, being perpetually exposed to the risk of a suit, which may ruin his reputation as well as his fortune. It becomes lawyers, therefore, to consider, when called upon to institute such suits, that little value can be placed on the *ipse dixit* of a layman sitting as critic upon the professional conduct of a physician. And that, aside from such personal delinquencies as drunkenness, or gross negligence, cruelty towards, or abandonment of his patient, the field in which the physician discharges his professional duties is practically *terra incognita* to the unlearned, and one where no lay critic can follow him " (*v*).

The same critic points out that the majority of suits for malpractice have been brought against surgeons and not against physicians. " Failure is rarely excused in a surgeon. He is expected to be an adroit medical carpenter who, with knife and saw and splint, can so re-construct the fractured or disjointed members of the human body as to leave no mark or line as evidence of their previous disrup-

---

(*u*) *Fawcett* v. *Mothersell*, 14 C. P. (Ont.) 104; *Jackson* v. *Hyde*, 28 U. C. R. 295.

(*v*) Ordronaux, sec. 54.

tion. On the other hand, the physician, enshrined within the penetralia of his mystic art, and mounted upon a Delphic tripod, inaccessible to vulgar criticism, pronounces his diagnosis and formulizes his prescriptions with unquestioned judgment. His diagnosis may be faulty, his medicines ill-selected, or ill-timed in their administration, and still no blame be incurred by him for any evil consequences that may ensue. For who will presume to say, in case of the patient's death, that he had not naturally reached that last illness foreordained to all men, and of which the physician's unsuccessful treatment is only official testimony? Who knows, in fact, when a man has reached his last illness until he dies? * * * And, as a corollary to this, strange as it may seem, one might, through unskilfulness, sacrifice a human life with more impunity than he could mutilate or deform a toe or a finger " (w).

The question of the amount of damages for personal injuries arising from malpractice is one resting a good deal in the discretion of the jury, and must of necessity be more or less uncertain. The party must recover all his damages, present and prospective, in one action. If the damages are so excessive as to strike all mankind, at first blush, as beyond all measure unreasonable and outrageous, and such as manifestly show the jury to have been actuated by passion, partiality, corruption, or prejudice, the court will grant a new trial. Sometimes, however, courts have granted new trials for excessive damages where the excessiveness has fallen short of this.

In considering what should be taken into account by a jury estimating the amount of damages to be awarded, the American courts have held, that the loss of time caused by the injury is to be considered (x). Also, the age and

(w) Ordronaux, sec. 86.
(x) *Jones* v. *Northmore*, 46 Vt. 587.

situation in life of the injured one, the expenses incurred, the permanent effect upon the plaintiff's capacity to pursue his professional calling, or to support himself as beforetimes, are essential factors (*y*).

Bodily pain, too, is to be considered and compensated for; and so much of mental suffering as may be indivisibly connected with it; but mental anguish and agony cannot be measured by money—the courts consider—and there is no established rule authoritatively commanding such a futile effort (*z*). In fact, the courts say, that one should get compensation for all the injuries that are the legal, direct, and necessary results of the malpractice (*a*).

The late case of *Phillips* v. *The South Western Railway Company* fully enunciates what, in the estimation of the English Judges, are to be considered in fixing the damages. Cockburn, C.J., said, that the heads of damages were the bodily injuries sustained, the pain undergone, the effect on the health of the sufferer, according to its degree and its probable duration as likely to be temporary or permanent, the expenses incidental to attempts to effect a cure, and the pecuniary loss sustained through inability to attend to a profession or business (*b*). In the Court of Appeal, Bramwell, L.J., remarked, "You must give the plaintiff a compensation for his pecuniary loss, you must give him compensation for his pain and bodily suffering. Of course, it is almost impossible to give an injured man what can be strictly called compensation, but you must take a reasonable view of the case, and must consider, under all the circumstances, what is a fair amount to be awarded to

---

(*y*) *Whalen* v. *St. Louis, etc., Ry.*, 60 Mo. 323; *Indianapolis, etc., Ry.* v. *Gaston*, 58 Ind. 224; *Leighton* v. *Sargent*, 11 Foster, N. H. 120.

(*z*) *Johnson* v. *Wills*, 6 Nev. 224.

(*a*) *Curtis* v. *Rochester & S. Ry.* 20 Barb. 282.

(*b*) L. R., 4 Q. B. D. 407.

him"(c). Phillips, who was a physician of middle age and robust health, making £5,000 a year, was so injured by a railway company, that he was totally unable to attend to his business; his life was a burden and a source of utmost pain, and the probablity was that he would never recover. The jury gave him £16,000, and the court refused to consider it excessive.

A physician, who has received personal injuries, may recover damages for loss of business as a physician, although he has not such a degree as would entitle him to maintain an action for professional services (d). The value of the fees which he would have received without suit may be estimated.

An action cannot be maintained against the representatives of a deceased surgeon to recover damages arising from the unskilful treatment of a patient. Such actions do not survive (e).

A medical practitioner who causes the death of a patient by such malpractice or negligence as would have entitled the patient (if death had not ensued) to maintain an action and recover damages against him in respect of the injury sustained thereby, is liable to an action for damages, notwithstanding the death of the patient, and although the circumstances under which the death was caused amount to felony. Such action may be brought for the benefit of the wife, husband, parent and child of the deceased, and the jury may give such damages as they may think proportioned to the injury resulting from such death to the parties respectively for whom and for whose benefit such

(c) L. R., 5 C. P. D. 280.
(d) *Holmes* v. *Halde*, 74 Me. 28.
(e) *Jenkins* v. *French*, 58 N. H. 532 ; Broom's Maxims, 702. But see *Hegerich* v. *Keddie*, 32 Hun, 141 ; *Yertore* v. *Wiswall*, 16 How. Pr. 8.

action is brought; but such injury must be a pecuniary loss, and the jury may not give damages as a *solatium* (*f*). In some of the American cases the mental anguish caused by the injury has been taken into account in estimating the damages to be given (*g*).

Not more than one action, however, will lie for and in respect of the same subject-matter of complaint, and every such action must be commenced within twelve months after the death of the person injured.

(*f*) Lord Campbell's Act, 9 & 10 Vict. cap. 93 ; R. S O. cap. 128 ; *Lett* v. *St. Lawrence & Ottawa Rw.*, 1 Ont. Rep. 545 ; *Blake* v. *Midland Rw.*, 18 Q. B. 93 ; *Bradburn* v. *G. W. R.*, L. R., 10 Ex. 3.

(*g*) *Morse* v. *Auburn & S. Rw.*, 10 Barb. 623.

## CHAPTER VI.

### CRIMINAL MALPRACTICE.

Whenever death ensues as the alleged consequence of malpractice it becomes necessary to inquire into the conduct of the physician, so as to determine how far his want of skill, or negligence, has conspired to produce it. The offence may, under certain circumstances indicating a wanton and malicious disregard of human life, amount to murder. Of course, a medical practitioner who should intentionally, and with malice, cause the death of a patient, would be held guilty of this crime; but in no case will an indictment for murder lie, unless there be a felonious destruction of life, with malice either express or implied. If a patient die from want of competent skill or sufficient attention the practitioner is guilty of manslaughter (*a*). "If one that is of the mystery of a physician take upon him the cure of a man, and giveth him such physic so as he dieth thereof, without any felonious intent and against his will, it is no homicide." So saith my Lord Coke. Blackstone says, "This is neither murder nor manslaughter, but misadventure, and he shall not be punished criminally." On the one hand, we must be careful and most anxious to prevent people from tampering in physic so as to trifle with the life of man; and on the other hand, we must take care not to charge criminally a person who is of general skill because he has been unfortunate in a particular case. It is God who gives, man only administers, medicine; and the medicine

(*a*) Glenn, p. 259.

that the most skilful may administer may not be productive of the expected effect; but it would be a dreadful thing if a man were to be called in question, criminally, whenever he happened to miscarry in his practice. It would be most fatal to the efficiency of the medical profession if no one could administer medicine without a halter round his neck (*b*).

At one time it was held, that if one, not a regular physician or surgeon, should adminster a medicine or perform an operation with a fatal effect, it would be manslaughter at the least; but long since, by Sir Matthew Hale, (one of the greatest Judges that ever adorned the English Bench), this doctrine was questioned (*c*). Now, however, both in England and America, it is well settled that it makes no difference whether the party be a regular practitioner or not; if he, *bona fide* and honestly exercising his best skill to cure a patient, performs an operation or administers a medicine which causes the patient's death he is not guilty of manslaughter. "God forbid," saith Lord Hale, "that any mischance of this kind should make a person not licensed, guilty of murder or manslaughter. This doctrine, that if any one dies under the hand of an unlicensed physician, it is felony, is apochryphal and fitted, I fear, to gratify and flatter doctors and licentiates in physic; though it may have its use, to make people cautious and wary how they take upon themselves too much, in this dangerous employment." Hullock, B., remarked that it would be most dangerous for it to get abroad that if an operation should fail the surgeon would be liable to be prosecuted for manslaughter. And as to making a difference between regular and irregular practitioners the same learned Judge aptly put it, "in remote parts of the country many persons would be left to die if

---

(*b*) *R.* v. *Long*, 4 C. & P. 398; *R.* v. *Crick*, 1 F. & F. 519.
(*c*) 4 Coke Inst. 251; 4 Bla. Com. 197; 1 Hale, P. C. 429.

irregular surgeons were not allowed to practise." Or as another Judge put it, we should have many of the poorer sort of people die for want of help, lest their intended helpers might miscarry (d).

Lord Lyndhurst agrees with the rule, but makes an exception. He says, "I agree that in these cases there is no difference between a licensed physician or surgeon and a person acting as a physician or surgeon without a license. In either case if a party having a competent degree of skill and knowledge makes an accidental mistake in the treatment of a patient, through which mistake death ensues, he is not thereby guilty of manslaughter; but if, where proper medical assistance can be had, a person, totally ignorant of the science of medicine, takes on himself to administer a violent and dangerous remedy to one labouring under disease, and death ensues in consequence of that dangerous remedy having been so administered, then he is guilty of manslaughter." Webb, a publican, had given large doses of Morrison's pills to one ill of small-pox (e).

"If any one, whether he be a regular or licensed medical man or not, professes to deal with the life or health of others, he is bound to have competent skill to perform the task that he holds himself out to perform, and he is bound to treat his patient with care, attention and assiduity;" and if the patient dies for want of either, the practitioner is guilty of manslaughter. "Every person who enters into a learned profession undertakes to bring to the exercise of it a reasonable degree of care and skill" (f). And if a medical man, though lawfully qualified to act as such, cause

(d) *Rex* v. *Van Butchell*, 3 C. & P. 629; *Rice* v. *The State*, 8 Mo. 561; *Com.* v. *Thompson*, 6 Mass. 134.

(e) *Rex* v. *Webb*, 1 M. & Rob. 405. See also *Rex* v. *Simpson*, 4 C. & P. 407 n.

(f) Bolland, B., in *Rex* v. *Spiller*, 5 C. & P. 19; *Lamphier* v. *Philpot*, per Tindal, C.J., 8 C. & P. 575.

the death of a person by the grossly unskilful or grossly incautious use of a dangerous instrument, he is guilty of manslaughter. No one is justified in making use of an instrument, in itself a dangerous one, unless he does so with a proper degree of skill and caution (*g*). There must be competent knowledge and care in dealing with a dangerous drug; if a man is ignorant of the nature of the drug he uses, or is guilty of gross want of care in its use, it would be criminal culpability (*h*). In Iowa, it was held that one assuming to act as a physician, who treats a patient in good faith and to the best of his ability, is not criminally responsible for the death of his patient, caused by the medicine he administers (*i*).

"To substantiate the charge of manslaughter, the prisoner must have been guilty of criminal misconduct, arising either from the grossest ignorance, or the most criminal inattention; one or other of these is necessary to make him guilty of that criminal negligence and misconduct which is essential to make out a case of manslaughter." Thus Lord Ellenborough laid down the law in the case of a man midwife who was on his trial for murder by malpractice (*j*). Long since in the *Mirror* (*k*) it was said, "If physicians or chirurgeons take upon them a cure, and have no knowledge or skill therein, or if they have knowledge, if nevertheless they neglect the cure, or minister that which is cold for hot, or take little care thereof, or neglect due diligence therein, and especially in burning and cutting off members, which they are forbidden to do, but at the peril of their patient, if their patients die or lose their members; in such cases they are manslayers or mayhemdors." Park, J.,

---

(*g*) Per Coleridge, J.; *Rex v. Spilling*, 2 M. & Rob. 107.
(*h*) *R. v. Chamberlaine*, 10 Cox, C. C. 486; Blackburn, J.
(*i*) *State v. Shulz*, 55 Ia. 628.
(*j*) *Rex v. Williamson*, 3 C. & P. 635; 14 Eng. Com. Law Rep. 297.
(*k*) Cap. 4, sec. 16.

charged the jury very similarly in one of St. John Long's celebrated cases. "If," said his Lordship, "you think there was gross ignorance or scandalous inattention in the conduct of the prisoner, then you will find him guilty; if you do not think so, then your verdict will be otherwise" (*l*).

Wharton considers that the position assumed by Lord Ellenborough depends upon the honesty and *bona fides* of the practitioner; and that if he is pursuing a plan of bold imposture the law would be otherwise (*m*).

In Long's case, Baron Garrow said, "I make no distinction between the person who consults the most eminent physician and the cases of those whose necessities or whose folly may carry them into any other quarter. It matters not whether the individual consulted be the President of the College of Surgeons, or the humblest bone-setter of the village; but, be it one or the other, he ought to bring into the case ordinary skill and diligence. I am of opinion that if a person who has ever so much or so little skill sets my leg and does it as well as he can and does it badly, he is excused; but, suppose the person comes drunk, and gives me a tumbler full of laudanum, and sends me into the other world, is it not manslaughter? And why is that? Because I have a right to have reasonable care and caution." In a subsequent case against the same practitioner, Bayley, B., said to the jury, "I have no hesitation in saying for your guidance, that if a man be guilty of gross neglect in attending to his patient after he has applied a remedy, or of gross rashness in the application of it, and death ensues in consequence, he will be liable to a conviction for manslaughter." "I consider rashness will be sufficient to make it manslaughter. As, for instance, if I have the toothache, and a person undertakes to cure it by

(*l*) *Rex* v. *St. John Long*, 4 C. & P. 378; 19 Eng. Com. Law Rep. 404.
(*m*) Wharton on Homicide, sec. 148.

administering laudanum, and says, 'I have no notion how much will be sufficient,' but gives one a cupful, which immediately kills; or if a person prescribing James' powder says, 'I have no notion how much should be taken,' and yet gives one a tablespoonful, which has the same effect; such persons, acting with rashness, will, in my opinion, be guilty of manslaughter. A prosecution is for the public benefit, and the willingness of the patient cannot take away the offence against the public" (*n*).

The matter has been well put in a Missouri case. "If," said the Judge, "the party prescribing has so much knowledge of the fatal tendency of the prescription that it may reasonably be presumed that he administered the medicine from an obstinate and wilful rashness, and not from an honest intention and expectation of effecting a cure, he is guilty of manslaughter at least, though he might not have intended any bodily harm to the patient "(*o*). It is the presence of intention which determines the moral complexion of an action, and whenever this intention (always presumed to be good) is proved to be bad, then, and then only, does a physician become criminally responsible for his wrongdoings. Doubtless, a bad intention may be at times inferred from the character of the misconduct; and neglect, particularly when gross, may be classed among those reasons which justify such an inference (*p*).

What the law deems gross negligence has been thus defined in a case where a "Herbalist" was on trial for manslaughter, for the death of a patient through an overdose of colchium seeds and brandy for a cold. "Gross negligence might be of two kinds; in one sense, where a man, for instance, went hunting, and neglected his patient,

---

(*n*) *Rex* v. *St. John Long*, 4 C. & P. 423; 19 E. C. L. R. 440.

(*o*) *Rice* v. *The State*, 8 Mo. 561.

(*p*) Ordronaux, secs. 80, 77. But see *R.* v. *Nancy Simpson*, 4 C. & P. 407 n.

who died in consequence. Another sort of gross negligence consisted in rashness, where a person was not sufficiently skilled in dealing with dangerous medicines which should be carefully used, of the properties of which he was ignorant, or how to administer a proper dose. A person who, with ignorant rashness, and without skill in his profession, used such a dangerous medicine, acted with gross negligence. It was not, however, every slip that a man might make that rendered him liable to a criminal investigation. It must be a substantial thing. If a man knew that he was using medicines beyond his knowledge and was meddling with things above his reach, that was culpable rashness. Negligence might consist in using medicines in the use of which care was required, and of the properties of which the person using them was ignorant. A person who so took a leap in the dark in the administration of medicines, was guilty of gross negligence. If a man was wounded and another man applied to his wound sulphuric acid, or something which was of a dangerous nature, and ought not to be applied, and which led to fatal results, then the person who applied this remedy would be answerable, and not the person who inflicted the wound, because a new cause had supervened. But, if the person who dressed the wound applied a proper remedy, then, if a fatal result ensued, he who inflicted the wound remained liable." In these words Willes, J., charged the jury, and they, after a long deliberation, brought in a verdict of "not guilty" (*q*). And in the very recent case of *State* v. *Hardister* (*r*), it was held that a physician is criminally liable for his gross ignorance causing the death of his patient, but not for a mere mistake of judgment.

However, in the celebrated case against the father and founder of the botanic or steam system of medicine, whose

(*q*) *Rex* v. *Markuss*, 4 F. & F. 356.
(*r*) 38 Ark. 605.

favorite remedies were coffee, "well-my-gristle," and "ram cats," it was held, that if a person assuming to be a physician, through gross ignorance, but honestly and *bona fide*, administers medicine which causes the death of the patient, he is not guilty of manslaughter (*s*). This was in the year 1809; and the doctrine laid down was followed in 1844 in Missouri in an exactly similar case (*t*). And quite recently in Iowa, where one Shulz was tried for manslaughter because his patient died under the Baunscheidt practice, *i. e.*, pricking the body and rubbing in a certain kind of oil, the Court on review said: "In 2 Bishop's Criminal Law, (4th Ed.) sec. 695, the law upon this subject is declared as follows: 'From the relationship of physician and patient the death of the latter not unfrequently arises. On this subject the doctrine seems to have been held that whenever one undertakes to cure another of disease or to perform on him a surgical operation, he renders himself thereby liable to the criminal law, if he does not carry to his duty some degree of skill, though what degree may not be clear; consequently, if the patient dies through his ill-treatment, he is indictable for manslaughter. On the other hand, a more humane doctrine is laid down, that since it is lawful and commendable for one to cure another, if he undertakes this office in good faith and adopts the treatment he deems best, he is not liable to be adjudged a felon, though the treatment should be erroneous, and in the eyes of those who assume to know all about this subject, which in truth is understood by no mortal, grossly wrong, and though he is a person called, by those who deem themselves wise, grossly ignorant of medicine and surgery. The former doctrine seems to be the English one, and so in England a person, whether a licensed medical practitioner or not, who undertakes to deal with the life or health of

---

(*s*) *Com. v. Thompson*, 6 Mass. 134.
(*t*) *Rice v. State*, 8 Mo. 561.

people, is bound to have competent skill or suffer criminally for the defect. Now, if a man thinks he has competent skill, and makes no misrepresentation to his patients concerning the amount or kind of medical education actually received by himself, he seems in reason to stand on exactly the foundation occupied by every person who honestly undertakes medical practice after full advantages, so far as concerns his state of mind, and it is the mind to which we look in questions of legal guilt. Any person undertaking a cure, but being grossly careless and thus producing death, is for a different reason liable to a charge of manslaughter, whether he is a licensed practitioner or not.' These cases seem to us to announce a correct rule. The interests of society will be subserved by holding a physician civilly liable in damages for the consequences of his ignorance, without imposing upon him criminal liability when he acts with good motives and honest intentions "(*u*).

If the death of a man has been accelerated by the want of due skill and competency, or by the carelessness, of his physician, the latter cannot defend himself by proving that his patient was afflicted with a mortal disease (*v*). If a man who has received a serious wound is placed under the charge of a surgeon who, in probing the wound or otherwise operating on the patient, immediately causes his death ; then, if the surgeon has acted negligently, or maliciously, he is indictable for the homicide, and the original assailant only for an attempt. But, if the surgeon using due skill and care occasions death while he is endeavouring to heal the wound, then he who inflicted the wound is chargeable with the death ; for he who does an unlawful act is responsible for all the consequences that in the ordinary course of events flow from it. It is an ordinary consequence of a wound that a surgeon should be called in to attend to it,

(*u*) 55 Iowa, 698.
(*v*) *R.* v. *Webb*, 1 M. & R. 405; Wharton on Homicide, sec. 405.

and it is a necessary incident of surgery that patients should die under the knife. It is no defence, where a death is not shewn to have been produced by the medical attendant's negligence, that the deceased might have recovered if a higher degree of professional skill had been employed (*w*).

If a person is assailed by a fatal disease, and there is no escape from it, save by a dangerous surgical operation, then, if he gives his free and intelligent consent to the operation, and it is skilfully performed, the surgeon cannot be blamed even though the patient perish under the knife. The German Jurists go still further and say, suppose a dangerous operation is required as the last hope of resuscitating an unconscious person; if the operation is performed with the skill usual to surgeons under such circumstances, and death ensue, the surgeon is blameless (*x*). If a woman is in such a state of labor that her life can only be preserved by the sacrifice of that of the child, then it is not only the right but the duty of the attendant to save the mother at the expense of the babe. Wharton says that this position is indisputable (*y*).

From the leading cases the following propositions may be extracted, say Wharton and Stillè, sec. 1068.

1. If the defendant acted honestly and used his best skill to cure, and it does not appear that he thrust himself in the place of a competent person, it makes no difference whether he was at the time a regular physician or surgeon, or not.

2. To constitute guilt, gross ignorance or negligence must be proved.

(*w*) *R.* v. *Lee*, 4 F. & F. 63; *Com.* v. *McPike*, 3 Cush. 181; *Com.* v. *Hackett*, 2 Allen, 137; Wharton on Homicide, sec. 385.
(*x*) Wharton on Homicide, sec. 554.
(*y*) Wharton on Homicide, sec. 557.

3. A defendant who, with competent knowledge, makes a mistake in a remedy is not answerable, but it is otherwise when a violent remedy, shewn to have occasioned death, is administered by a person grossly ignorant but with average capacity, in which case malice is presumed in the same way that it is presumed when a man *compos mentis* lets loose a mad bull into a thoroughfare, or casts down a log of wood on a crowd.

4. Where competent medical aid can be had, the application of violent remedies by an ignorant person, though with the best motives, involves him in criminal responsibility.

5. Express malice, or an intent to commit a personal or social wrong, makes the practitioner criminally responsible in all cases of mischief.

These well known writers say, that according to Caspar and Böcker, in the treatment of internal diseases, the physician can never be held guilty of criminal carelessness for failing to use any particular remedy, since there is never any remedy upon which all authorities are agreed, and since it is always possible the patient may recover without the use of such remedy (z).

(z) Medical Jurisprudence, sec. 1059.

## CHAPTER VII.

### PROFESSIONAL EVIDENCE.

It was decided nearly one hundred years ago, in the Duchess of Kingston's case, that a medical man has no privilege to avoid giving in evidence any statement made to him by a patient, but that he is bound to disclose, when called upon to do so in a court of justice, every communication, however private and confidential, which has been made to him by a patient while attending him in a professional capacity (*a*). This has often been deemed a grievance by medical men, and considered a compulsory breach of professional ethics; for the relations between patient and physician, being necessarily of a confidential character, communications made to a physician are looked upon, by the profession, as confessions which should be kept religiously locked in the brain of the physician. Lord Mansfield said, "If a medical man was voluntarily to reveal those secrets, to be sure he would be guilty of a breach of honour and of great indiscretion, but to give that information which by the law of the land he is bound to do will never be imputed to him as any indiscretion whatever" (*b*).

A French writer says, the tribunals neither ought, nor have they the power, to exact from a physician the revelation of a secret confided to him because of his office; at all events, he may and ought to refuse to tell. Religion,

---

(*a*) *Duchess of Kingston's Case*, 20 Howell St. Tr. 573; *Wilson* v. *Rastall*, 4 T. R. 760; *Greenough* v. *Gaskill*, 1 Myl. & K. 103; *R.* v. *Gibbons*, 1 C. & P. 97; *Broad* v. *Pitt*, 3 C. & P. 579.

(*b*) *Duchess of Kingston's Case*, supra.

probity, nay, the rights of society, make this the law. Still more are we bound to secrecy when not compelled to disclose. Upon this point casuists and jurisconsults are of one opinion (c).

These communications between physician and patient, which may relate to the history of a transaction in which a wound has been received, or a particular disease communicated, whenever essential to the treatment of the patient's case, are in some States of the American Union considered privileged communications, which the physician is either expressly forbidden, or not obliged, to reveal. This is the law in Arkansas, California, Indiana, Michigan, Iowa, Missouri, Minnesota, Montana, New York, Ohio and Wisconsin. In Wisconsin he is not compelled, and in the other States named he is not allowed to make the disclosure; but in Minnesota the prohibition extends only to civil cases; and in Iowa, Indiana and Minnesota, the seal can be removed by the patient himself. In these States the confession, in order to be protected against disclosure, must relate exclusively to such matters as are indispensable to the professional treatment of the patient. Communications made outside of this sphere acquire no immunity from having been entrusted to physicians, for at common law such are not deemed privileged, and wherever so recognized they are the creatures of statutory enactment (d).

As stated, in some of the above-mentioned States, the party interested may waive the privilege, in which case the communication may be disclosed (e). But in New York it is expressly enacted that "no person duly authorized to practise physic, or surgery, shall be allowed to disclose any information which he may have acquired in attending any

(c) Belloc. Cours de Med. leg. 17.
(d) 1 Greenleaf on Evidence, sec. 248; *Campan* v. *North*, 39 Mich. 606.
(e) *Harris* v. *Russel*, 16 Ind. 209; *Staunton* v. *Parker*, 19 Hun. 55; *Fraser* v. *Jenneson*, 42 Mich. 206.

patient in a professional character, and which information was necessary to enable him to prescribe for such patient as a physician, or to do any act for him as a surgeon "(*f*).

Yet, even there, the statute will not be construed so as to shield a person charged with a crime, instead of being a protection to the victim, the patient (*g*).

The seal upon the physicians lips is not taken away by the patient's death (*h*).

Necessarily all communications to be privileged must be of a lawful character, and not against morality or public policy; hence a consultation as to the means of procuring an abortion on another is not privileged; nor, by parity of reason, would any similar conference which was held for the purpose of devising a crime or evading its consequences (*i*).

It must appear not only that the information was acquired during professional attendance, but was such as was necessary to enable the physician to prescribe. It is for the party objecting to shew that the information sought to be obtained is within the statutory exclusion. "It will not do to extend the rule of exclusion so far as to embarrass the administration of justice. It is not even all information which comes within the letter of the statute which is to be excluded. The exclusion is aimed at confidential communications of a patient to his physician, and also such information as a physician may acquire of secret ailments by an examination of the person of his patient. The policy of the statute is to enable a patient, without danger of exposure, to disclose to his physician all inform-

---

(*f*) 2 N. Y. Rev. St. 406, sec. 73; *Hunn* v. *Hunn*, 1 Thomp. & C. 499.

(*g*) *Pierson* v. *People*, 79 N. Y. 434.

(*h*) *Cohen* v. *Continental, etc., Ins. Co.*, 41 N. Y. Super. Ct. 296; *Grattan* v. *Metropolitan L. Ins. Co.*, 80 N. Y. 281.

(*i*) *Hewitt* v. *Prime*, 21 Wend. 79.

ation necessary for his treatment. Its purpose is to invite confidence and to prevent a breach thereof. Suppose a patient has a fever, or a fractured leg or skull, or is a raving maniac, and these ailments are obvious to all about him, may not the physician who is called to attend him testify to these matters?" "Before information sought to be obtained from physicians, witnesses can be excluded. The court must know somewhat of the circumstances under which it was acquired, and must be able to see that it is within both the language and the policy of the law" (*j*).

A report of the medical officer of an insurance company on the health of a party proposing to insure his life is not privileged from production; nor is the report of a surgeon of a railway company, as to the injuries sustained by a passenger in an accident, unless such a report has been obtained with a view to impending litigation (*k*).

Representations made by a sick person of the nature and effects of the malady under which he is suffering are receivable as original evidence, whether made to a physician or to any other; though, if made to a physician, they are entitled to greater weight than if made to a man incapable of forming a correct judgment respecting the accuracy of the statements, from unacquaintance with the symptoms of diseases (*l*). When the bodily or mental feelings of a party are to be proved, his exclamations or expressions indicating present pain or malady are competent evidence (*m*); and

---

(*j*) *Edington* v. *Ætna Life Ins. Co.*, 77 N. Y. 564, but see *Edington* v. *Ætna Life Ins. Co.*, 67 N. Y. 185.

(*k*) *Lee* v. *Hammerton*, 10 L. T.; N. S. 730; *Mahony* v. *Nat. Widow's Life Assurance Fund*, L. R. 6 C. P. 252; *Baker* v. *London & S. W. Railway*, L. R. 3 Q. B. 91; *Cossey* v. *L. B. & C.*, L. R. 5 C. P. 146; *Skinner* v. *G. N. R.*, L. R. 9 Ex. 298.

(*l*) *Aveson* v. *Lord Kinnaird*, 6 East 188; Taylor on Evidence, secs. 580, 581, 7th ed.

(*m*) *Bacon* v. *Charlton*, 7 Cush. 586; *Chapen* v. *Marlborough*, 9 Gray 244; *Barber* v. *Merriam*, 11 Allen 322.

the complaints and statements of the injured party, if made at the very time of the occurrence, are admissible as *res gestæ*, not only as to the bodily suffering, but as to the circumstances of the occurrence; and the time in question is not the time of injury, but the time when it is material to prove a condition of bodily or mental suffering, and that may be material for weeks, and perhaps months, after an injury has been inflicted. The statements are admissible even though made after the commencement of an action, though this may be a circumstance to detract from the weight of the evidence of a physician, so far as it was founded on the statements (*n*). But statements or declarations of a sick or injured person, referring to his state and condition at a time past, and not furnishing evidence of a present existing malady, are to be carefully excluded, whether made to an expert or a non-expert (*o*), and statements in writing by patients to a medical man, describing the symptoms of the illness upon which the physician has advised the patient, are also inadmissible in evidence (*p*). It has been said in Illinois, that as a physician must necessarily, in forming his opinion, be, to some extent, guided by what the sick person may have told him in detailing his pains and sufferings, not only the opinion of the expert, founded in part upon such data, is receivable in evidence, but that he may state what the patient said in describing his bodily condition, if said under circumstances which free it from all suspicions of being spoken with reference to future litigation and give it the character of *res gestae* (*q*).

(*n*) *Kennard* v. *Burton*, 25 Me. 39; *Gray* v. *McLaughlin*, 26 Ia. 279; *Brown* v. *N. Y. C.*, 32 N. Y. 597; *Caldwell* v. *Murphy*, 11 N. Y. 344; *Barber* v. *Merriam*, sup.; *Denton* v. *State*, 1 Swan 279; *Matteson* v. *N. Y. C.*, 35 N. Y. 487.

(*o*) *Chapin* v. *Malborough*, sup.; *Lush* v. *McDaniel*, 13 Ired. L. 485; *Rogers* v. *Cain*, 30 Tex. 284; *Wilson* v. *Granby*, 47 Conn.

(*p*) *Witt* v. *Witt*, 3 Sw. & Trist. 143.

(*q*) *Ill. Cen. R. R.* v. *Sutton*, 42 Ill. 438.

On the other hand, in Massachusetts, in an action for personal injuries, a surgeon who had attended plaintiff was held competent to testify as to plaintiff's condition from what he saw, but not from anything the patient told him (*r*). A physician testified that the plaintiff stated she had received a blow in the stomach. The Court said that it would clearly have been competent for the physician, after having testified to the plaintiff's condition and to the complaints and symptoms of pain and sufferings stated by her, to have given his opinion that they were such as might have been expected to follow the infliction of a severe blow. But it was not competent for the physician to testify to her statement that she had received a blow in her stomach (*s*). And in Tennessee, the statement made by a man when his wounds were being examined, as to who made them, or as to the instrument with which they were inflicted, was deemed inadmissible (*t*).

Memoranda, although not legal instruments in the proper sense of the term, have been considered as an inferior class of records, and as such entitled to some standing in courts. Such minutes of past facts may be used by experts while under examination, but only to refresh their memory, and not to take its place. For this purpose they may use written entries in note books, or even copies of them, provided always they can swear to the truth of the facts as there stated. Yet, if they can not from recollection speak to the fact any farther than as finding it stated in a written entry, their testimony will amount to nothing. It is not necessary that the writing should have been made by the expert himself, nor even that it should be an original writ-

---

(*r*) *Rowell* v. *Lowell*, 11 Gray 420.
(*s*) *Roosa* v. *Boston Loan Co.*, 132 Mass. 439; *Quaife* v. *C. & N. W. R.*, 48 Wis. 513.
(*t*) *Denton* v. *State*, 1 Swan 279.

ing, provided, after inspecting it, he can testify to the facts from his own recollection (*u*).

The English and American authorities agree that medical, or other scientific books, are not competent evidence in courts of law; they cannot be put in evidence, although the medical witnesses state that such books are works of authority in medicine. Tindal, C.J., thought that witnesses might be asked whether in the course of their reading they had found such-and-such a rule laid down; they might be asked how far their opinion was founded on books, and might refer to such books; they might be asked their judgment on the point, and the grounds of it, which may be in some degree founded on these books, as a part of their general knowledge, but the book itself could not be read. And as late as 1875, Mr. Justice Brett refused to allow Taylor's Medical Jurisprudence to be read to the jury, saying: "That is no evidence in a court of justice. It is a mere statement by a medical man of hearsay facts of cases at which he was, in all probability, not present. I cannot allow it to be read." And the refusal seems to be the rule in England. And Redfield, C.J., says, that when objected to, these books have not generally been allowed to be read in the United States, either to the Court or jury. And a a very recent writer says, "The result of the cases on this subject shews clearly that the very decided weight of authority is against the admissibility in evidence of standard medical treatises." Such is the rule in England, Ontario, Indiana, Maine, Maryland, Massachusetts, Michigan, North Carolina, Rhode Island and Wisconsin, supported by *dicta* in California and New Hampshire, and opposed by decisions in Alabama and Iowa (*v*).

(*u*) Greenleaf on Evid. sec. 436; Ordronaux sec. 124; Glenn, p. 284.
(*v*) *Collier* v. *Simpson*, 5 C. & P. 73; *Reg.* v. *Thomas*, 13 Cox Cr. Cas. 77; Redfield on Wills, p. 145; *People* v. *Hall*, 48 Mich. 486; Rogers on Expert Evidence, sec. 180; *Brown* v. *Sheppard*, 13 U. C. R. 178.

In Iowa and Wisconsin such books have been allowed to be read, the Court in one case remarking, "The opinion of an author, as contained in his works, we regard as better evidence than the mere statement of those opinions by a witness, who testifies as to his recollection of them from former reading. Is not the latter secondary to the former? On the whole, we think it the safest rule to admit standard medical books as evidence of their opinions upon questions of medical skill or practice involved in the treatment." In Wisconsin, however, the court seems now to have overruled its earlier decisions, and to have sided with the majority (*w*).

In Illinois, a witness may, to test his knowledge, be cross-examined as to his reading of particular authors upon the subject, and as to whether reputable writers do not entertain certain views upon the subject. Paragraphs from standard authors, treating of the disease in question, may be read to the witness, and he may be asked if he agrees therewith, as one of the means of testing his knowledge; but care should be taken by the court to confine such cross-examination within reasonable limits, and to see that the quotations read are fairly selected so as to present the author's views. Mr. Rogers questions the wisdom of this decision (*x*). The witness, however, cannot read from a scientific work in his examination in chief, though he be an expert and agree with the views expressed by the author (*y*). Nor can a passage from a book be got before a jury as evidence in an indirect manner, when it cannot be read to them. So it was decided where a medical man was asked if he was acquainted with a certain book; he replied, that he had heard of it, but had not read it. He was then asked

(*w*) *Bowman* v. *Woods*, 1 Ia. 44; *Luning* v. *State*, 1 Chandler (Wisc.) 264; *Ripon* v. *Bittel*, 30 Wisc. 362; *Stirling* v. *Thorp*, 54 Wisc.

(*x*) *Con. Mut. Life Ins. Co.* v. *Ellis*, 89 Ill. 516; Expert Testimony, sec. 182.

(*y*) *Com.* v. *Sturtevant*, 117 Mass. 123.

whether it was considered good authority, and he said it was. He was then asked to read a certain paragraph; this he did, and was re-called. Counsel then read from the book the same paragraph and asked if such a case as that stated was reported. Held to be error (z). And in Ontario it has been held improper to ask medical witnesses, on cross-examination, what books they consider best upon the subject in question, and then to read such books to the jury; but they may be asked whether such books have influenced their opinion (a).

Although, as a rule, scientific books cannot be read to a jury as evidence, they may be read to discredit the testimony of experts, who claim to be familiar with them and refer to them as authority. Where one borrows credit for his accuracy, by referring to books treating of the subject, and by implying that he echoes the standard authorities, the book may be resorted to, to disprove the statement of the witness, and to enable the jury to see that the book does not contain what he says it does, and thus to disparage the witness, and hinder the jury from being imposed upon by a false light (b). It has been held again and again that scientific books cannot be read by counsel to the jury as a part of their argument. Shaw, C.J., of Massachusetts, says, "Facts or opinions cannot be laid before the jury, except by the testimony under oath of persons skilled in such matters." Again, "where books are thus offered (i. e., to be read in argument), they are, in effect, used as evidence, and the substantial objection is, that they are statements wanting the sanction of an oath; and the statement thus proposed is made by one not present, and not liable to cross-examination. If the same author were cross-examined, and

---

(z) *Marshall* v. *Brown*, 15 N. W. Rep. 55.
(a) *Brown* v. *Sheppard*, 13 U. C. R. 178.
(b) *Pinncy* v. *Cohill*, 12 N. W. Rep. 862; *Ripon* v. *Bittell*, 30 Wisc. 362.

called to state the grounds of his opinions, he might, himself, alter or modify it, and it would be tested by a comparison with the opinions of others. Medical authors, like writers in other departments of science, have their various and conflicting theories, and often defend and sustain them with ingenuity. But as the whole range of medical literature is not open to persons of common experience, a passage may be found in one book favorable to a particular opinion, when, perhaps, the same opinion may have been vigorously contested, and, perhaps, triumphantly overthrown, by other medical authors, but authors whose works would not be likely to be known to counsel or client, or to Court or jury. Besides, medical science has its own nomenclature, its technical terms and words of art, and also common words used in a peculiar manner, distinct from the received meaning in the general use of the language. From these and other causes, persons not versed in medical literature, though having a good knowledge of the general use of the English language, would be in danger, without an interpreter, of misapprehending the true meaning of the author. Whereas a medical witness could not only give the fact of his opinion, and the grounds on which it is formed, with the sanction of his oath, but would also state and explain it in language intelligible to men of common experience. If it be said that no books should be read, except works of good and established authority, the difficulty at once arises as to the question, what constitutes "good authority?" (c).

In an English case, counsel, in addressing the jury, attempted to quote from a work on surgery; Alderson, B., would not allow him, saying, "You surely cannot contend that you may give the book in evidence, and if not, what right have you to quote from it in your address, and do that indirectly which you would not be permitted to do in

---

(c) *Ashworth* v. *Kittridge*, 12 Cush. 193.

the ordinary course?" In Massachusetts, North Carolina, Michigan, California and New York, similar decisions have been given (d); and in giving the dissenting opinion in *State and Hoyt* (e), Loomis, J., said, "Books may be crazy as well as men, and all sorts of theories relative to responsibility for crime are advocated in books. Courts do not take judicial notice of standard medical or scientific works, and the standard works of to-day may not long continue such, owing to new discoveries and advancing knowledge." In this case the question was as to reading medical books on insanity on trials where the question of insanity arose; the book was Ray's "Medical Jurisprudence of Insanity." In a a still later case (f), it was held to have been error for the attorney, on the argument, to read to the jury extracts from Brown's "Medical Jurisprudence of Insanity." The Court said, that it is peculiarly important that a defendant charged with a crime should be confronted by the expert witnesses against him, and that they should be cross-examined in his presence. But when the opinions of a writer are permitted to go to the jury, the writer is not sworn or cross-examined. If held admissible the question (of insanity) may be tried, not by the testimony, but upon excerpts from works presenting partial views of variant and perhaps contradictory theories (g).

In Connecticut, however, in a murder case the Court (Loomis, J., and Park, C.J., out of the five Judges dissenting,) held, that standard medical works on insanity might be read to the jury by the counsel for the accused, when

---

(d) *Reg.* v. *Crouch*, 1 Cox Cr. Cas. 94; *Washburn* v. *Cuddihy*, 8 Gray 430; *Huffman* v. *Click*, 77 N. C. 54; *Fraser* v. *Jennison*, 42 Mich. 206, 214; *People* v. *Wheeler*, 9 Pac. Coast L. J. 581; *Robinson* v. *N. Y. C.*, 24 A. L. J. 357.

(e) 46 Conn. 330.

(f) *People* v. *Wheeler*, 9 Pac. C. L. Jour. 581.

(g) See also *Collier* v. *Simpson*, 5 C. & P. 73; *Ordway* v. *Haynes*, 50 N. H. 159; *People* v. *Anderson*, 44 Cal. 65; *Carter* v. *State*, 2 Cart. 617; *Gale* v. *Rector*, 5 Bradw. 484; *Harris* v. *Panama R. Co.*, 3 Bosw. 7.

discussing the question of his insanity. It was said that "in this jurisdiction (that of Connecticut) for a long series of years counsel have been permitted to read to the jury, as a part of their argument upon this part of their case, extracts from such treatises as by the testimony of experts have been accepted by the profession as authority upon that subject, such treatises as have helped to form the opinion expressed by the expert. The practice by repetition has hardened into a rule"(h). In Indiana, it was held that if the extracts were merely argumentative and contained no opinions that could be regarded as properly matters of evidence, they might be admitted, subject to the instructions of the Court as to the law of the case and under the warning that they were not evidence. In Texas and in Delaware, similar decisions have been given (i). And in Ohio, where, at the trial of a cause, counsel was forbidden to read to the jury Youatt's work on Veterinary Surgery, the Court, on appeal, said, "It is not to be denied, but that a pertinent quotation or extract from a work on science or art, as well as from a classical, historical, or other publication, may, by way of argument or illustration, be not only admissible, but sometimes highly proper, and it would seem to make no difference whether it was repeated by counsel from recollection or read from a book. It would be an abuse of this privilege, however, to make it the pretence of getting improper matter before the jury as evidence in the cause." As it did not appear that the proposed quotation was relevant or came within the appropriate and legitimate scope of the argument, or that the party was injured by its exclusion, the Court would not reverse on this ground (j). Where the reading is allowed, it seems to be considered "a valuable privilege, yet so susceptible of abuse, that the

(h) *State* v. *Hoyt*, 46 Conn. 330.

(i) *Harvey* v. *State*, 40 Ind. 516; *Wade* v. *De Witt*, 20 Texas 398; *State* v. *West*, 1 Houston Cr. Cas. (Del.) 371.

(j) *Legg* v. *Drake*, 1 Ohio St. 286.

extent and manner of its exercise must be entrusted in a great measure to the sound discretion of the Court;"—"not a practice ever sanctioned directly or indirectly by the Court, nor one which has generally been considered by the Judges as of binding force in law, but rather as subject to the discretion which, it is true, has been usually exercised in favor of the accused in capital trials" (k).

Where the exclusion rule obtains, counsel in addressing the jury has no right to quote the opinions of medical men as given in their words; if they do, it is the duty of the Court to instruct the jury that such books are not in evidence but theories simply of medical men (l). But there is no question that, under all circumstances, books of science may be read in argument to the Court.

Medical men are often called to give evidence as to dying declarations where there is a charge of homicide, and where the cause of the death of the declarant is the subject of the declaration. They should remember that the declaration will not be admissible unless the deceased was conscious of approaching death and made it under a sense of his impending doom; any hope of recovery, however slight, renders the declaration inadmissible; and the question turns rather upon the expectation of death at the time of making the declaration than upon the interval between it and the death (m).

An entry made by a medical man, in the course of his profession, is admissible in evidence after his death, if it be against his interest; and such an entry will be received as evidence of collateral and independent matter, etc. When

---

(k) Per Loomis, J., *State* v. *Hoyt*, sup.; *Wade* v. *De Witt*, 20 Tex. 398, 400; *Luning* v. *State*, sup.; Experts and Expert Testimony by U. C. Moak, 24 A. L. J. 267.

(l) *Yoe* v. *State*, 49 Ill. 410.

(m) *Russell* on Crimes, 4th ed. vol. iii. p. 250.

the question was as to the age of a child, the book of the accoucheur who attended the mother was produced; it contained an entry as follows, "W. Fowden, Jun.'s, wife; *Filius circa hor.* 3 *post merid. nat.* etc. W. Fowden, 1768, April 22. *Filius natus* wife, £1 6s. 1d; Pd. 25 Oct. 1768." The word "Paid" was against the pecuniary interest of the accoucheur, so the entry was admitted to prove the date of the birth (*n*).

In England the rule is thus laid down as to excluding experts from the room during the examination of witnesses; "medical or other professional witnesses, who are summoned to give scientific opinions upon the circumstances of the case as established by other testimony, will be permitted to remain in court until this particular class of evidence commences, but then, like ordinary witnesses, they will have to withdraw, and to come in one by one, so as to undergo a separate examination." A similar rule prevails in Scotland and in the United States (*o*).

It would seem that the court has power to limit the number of experts in any case (*p*).

Taylor, in his well-known work on "Medical Jurisprudence," lays down many valuable suggestions for the guidance of medical witnesses; among other things, he says, "In reference to *facts*, a medical witness must bear in mind that he should not allow his testimony to be influenced by the consequences that may follow from his statement of them, or there probable effect on any case which is under trial. In reference to *opinions*, their possible influence on the fate of a prisoner should inspire caution in

---

(*n*) *Higham* v. *Ridgway*, 10 East 109.
(*o*) Taylor's Evid., vol. ii., sec. 1259; Alison's Criminal Law of Scotland, 542; Wharton's Evid., vol. i. p. 492.
(*p*) *Sizer* v. *Burt*, 4 Denio, 426; *Anthony* v. *Smith*, 2 Bos. (N.Y.) 503. 508; *Fraser* v. *Jameson*, 42 Mich. 206. 223.

forming them; but, when once formed, they should be honestly and candidly stated, without reference to consequences." "The questions put on either side should receive direct answers from the medical witness, and his manner should not be perceptibly different whether he is replying to a question put by the counsel for the prosecution, or for the defence." "The replies should be concise, distinct and audible, and except where explanation may be necessary, they should be confined strictly to the terms of the question." "Answers to questions should be neither ambiguous, undecided, nor evasive." "The replies should be made in simple language, free from technicality." "A medical witness may, without any imputation upon his *bona fides*, explain medical points to counsel, and correct him on medical subjects, when wrong in his views or statements, but he should avoid even the appearance of prompting counsel in the conduct of the case."

## CHAPTER VIII.

### MEDICAL EXPERTS.

Whenever the subject matter of a legal enquiry is such that, from its partaking of the nature of a science, art or trade, inexperienced persons are unlikely to prove capable of forming a correct judgment upon it without assistance, then the opinions of witnesses possessing peculiar skill and knowledge in the matters in question are admissible in courts of justice. And it is only when the matter inquired of lies within the range of the peculiar skill and experience of the witnesses, and is one of which the ordinary knowledge and experience of mankind does not enable them to see what inference should be drawn from the facts, that the skilled witnesses may supply opinions as their guide (a). The rule admitting the opinions of experts in such cases is founded on necessity, for juries are not selected with any view to their knowledge of a particular science, art or trade, requiring a course of previous study, experience or preparation (b).

The rule of law on which the giving in evidence the opinion of witnesses, who know nothing of the actual facts of the case, is founded, is not peculiar to medical testimony, but is as a general rule applicable to all cases where the question is one depending on skill and science in any particular department. . . . In general it is the opinion of the jury which is to govern, and this is to be formed upon the

---

(a) 1 Smith Lead. Cas., 6th Ed. 509; *Kennedy* v. *People*, 30 N. Y. 245.
(b) *Chicago, etc.*, v. *McGiven*, 78 Ill. 347; *Hartford Pro. Ins. Co.* v. *Harmer*, 20 Oh. St. 457.

proof of the facts laid before them. But some questions lie beyond the scope of the observation and experience of men in general, yet are quite within the observation and experience of those whose peculiar pursuits and profession have brought that class of facts frequently and habitually under their consideration. When, therefore, a question arises in a court of justice upon any such subject, and certain facts are proved by other witnesses, one skilled in such subject may be asked his opinion as to the character of such facts; or he may be asked his opinions on certain facts observed by himself. This is true with regard to any question of science, because persons conversant with such science have peculiar means, from a larger and more exact observation and long experience in such department of science, of drawing correct inferences from certain facts observed by themselves or testified to by other witnesses. The opinion of such witnesses is designed to aid the judgment of the jury in regard to the influence and effects of certain facts which lie out of the observation and experience of persons in general (c). These witnesses are called "experts." This term seems to imply both superior knowledge and practical experience in the art or profession. But generally nothing more is required to entitle one to give testimony as an expert, than that he has been educated in the particular art or profession; for persons are presumed to understand questions pertaining to their own profession or business (d).

The practice of admitting the evidence of experts is an old one: in the Roman Law they are frequently alluded to, and in the earliest Common Law reports they are spoken of as of established usage. Says Saunders, J., "and first I grant that if matters arise in our law which

(c) *Commonwealth* v. *Rodgers*, 7 Metc. 5, per Shaw, C.J.
(d) 1 Greenl. Evid., sec. 440; *Jones* v. *White*, 11 Hump. 268.

concern other sciences or faculties we commonly apply for the aid of that science or faculty which it concerns. In a case of mayhem the defendant prayed the court that the wound might be examined, on which a writ was issued to the sheriff to cause to come "*medicos chirurgos de melioribus London. ad informandum Dominum regem et curiam de his quæ eis exparte Domini Regis injungerentur* (e).

Some Judges and writers have very little respect for the evidence and opinions of experts. An Iowa Judge says, observation and experience "teach that the evidence of experts is of the very lowest order, and of the most unsatisfactory kind." One from Maine, speaks of "the vain babblings and oppositions of science so called, which swell the record of the testimony of experts when the hopes of a party depend rather upon mystification than enlightenment." An Illinois Judge quotes a distinguished occupant of the bench as saying, "if there was any kind of testimony not only of no value, but even worse than that, it was in his judgment that of medical experts." Lord Campbell said, "Hardly any weight is to be given to the evidence of what are called scientific witnesses: they come with a bias on their minds to support the cause in which they are embarked" (f). Taylor says, "Perhaps the testimony which least deserves credit with a jury is that of skilled witnesses. . . . Being zealous partisans their belief becomes synonymous with faith as defined by the apostle, and it too often is but the substance of things hoped for, the evidence of things not seen " (g). On the other hand, Best says, "It would not be easy to overrate the value of the evidence given in many difficult and delicate enquiries, not only by medical men and physiologists, but by learned

---

(e) Plowden, 125; Year Books, vol. v.

(f) *Whittaker* v. *Parker*, 42 Ia. 586; *State* v. *Watson*, 65 Me. 74; *Rutherford* v. *Morris*, 77 Ill. 404; *Tracy* Peerage, 10 Cl. & Fin. 191.

(g) Taylor on Evidence, sec. 50, Ed. 1872.

and experienced persons in various branches of science, art and trade " (h). And many Judges have spoken of the essential aid to courts and juries rendered by the opinion of the experienced, skilful and scientific witness who has a competent knowledge of the facts involved.

When one takes his place as an expert before a court, a legal paradox is instituted on his behalf, by which he is allowed to testify—not as to what he knows, but to what he believes or forms an opinion upon, based necessarily on probabilities of analogy as well as experience. Nothing is required (in the absence of any statutory provision to the contrary) to entitle any one to give evidence as a medical witness, than that he has been educated in the science of medicine; and this he may be by study without practice, or by practice without study; it is not necessary that he should be a physician, or have studied for one, nor be a graduate, nor one licensed to practise, nor need he be or have been a practitioner (i). One may be competent to testify as an expert, although his special knowledge of the particular subject of enquiry has been derived from the reading and study of standard authorities, and not from experience or actual observation. But one cannot qualify himself as an expert in a particular case merely by devoting himself to the study of authorities for the purposes of that case, when such reading and study is not in the line of his special calling or profession and is entered upon to enable him to testify in the case. In Vermont, however, it has been held that mere education as a physician, without some practice as such, is insufficient to qualify one as an expert; and in Arkansas, it is said, that competency must be shewn from study and experience. In New York, it has been held that one otherwise qualified, who is

---

(h) Best on Evidence, sec. 574.
(i) *State* v. *Wood*, 53 N. H. 484; *Masons* v. *Fuller*, 45 Vt. 29; *New Orleans, etc., Rw.* v. *Allbretton*, 38 Miss. 247; *Re Toomes*, 54 Cal. 515.

a physician and surgeon, may give evidence, although not in full practice at the time; this fact merely goes to affect his credit (*j*).

It is not necessary that the physician should have made the particular disease involved in the enquiry a specialty; medical men of practice and experience are experts, and their opinions are admissible in evidence upon questions that are strictly and legitimately embraced in their profession and practice. If one has made the matter in question a specialty, doubtless his opinion will be of more value than if he has not; and it has been said, that one who has devoted himself exclusively to one branch of his profession cannot give evidence as an expert on another (*k*). For example, one not an oculist may speak as to the cause of injuries to an eye; one who has not made diseases of the mind a special study may give his opinion as to the existence of insanity; one not a practical chemist or analyst, but understanding the practical details of chemistry and the means of detecting poisons, may testify as to the tests in the chemical analysis of a stomach, and as to the tests usually applied to detect poison (*l*). The law will even allow a physician to speak as to the length of time a mule has been suffering from a disease (*m*). But one who has had no experience as to the effect upon health of illuminating gas cannot testify in relation thereto as an expert (*n*). Nor can one who has for thirty years been exclusively treating the insane be permitted to testify, as an expert, on

---

(*j*) *Fairchild v. Bascomb*, 35 Vt. 410; *Polk v. State*, 36 Ark. 117; *Roberts v. Johnson*, 58 N. Y. 613.

(*k*) *Hathaway v. Nat. Life Ins. Co.*, 48 Vt. 335, 351; *Fairchild v. Bascomb*, supra.

(*l*) *Castner v. Sliker*, 33 N. J. (L.) 97; *State v. Reddick*, 7 Kan. 143; *State v. Henkle*, 6 Ia. 380; *State v. Cook*, 17 Kan. 391.

(*m*) *Horton v. Green*, 64 N. C. 64.

(*n*) *Emerson v. Lowell Gas Light Co.*, 6 Allen, 146.

the mental capacity of a person in the last stages of disease, who has not been previously insane (*o*).

To render the opinion of a witness competent evidence, he must, in general, be in some way peculiarly qualified to speak on the subject, and have knowledge not possessed by the mass of persons of ordinary experience and intelligence (*p*). Upon this principle, a priest who had studied physiology and psychology, in order that he might pass upon the mental conditions of communicants in his church, and who had so to decide daily, was permitted to speak as to the mental state of a woman whom he had attended in her last illness (*q*).

It is a question of fact to be decided at the trial, by the Court, whether a witness offered as an expert has the necessary qualification (*r*). And the matter cannot be referred to the decision of the jury. The decision of the Judge at the trial will not be interfered with by the Court, except in a clear and strong case (*s*).

Any one offered as an expert who cannot establish the fact of special knowledge or skill, in the particular department which he is called upon to illuminate, will be rejected. A Court before permitting an expert to testify may examine him, or hear evidence, to satisfy itself that the witness is really what he assumes to be (*t*).

(*o*) *Heald* v. *Wing*, 5 Me. 392.
(*p*) *Harris* v. *Panama R. R. Co.*, 3 Bosw. (N. Y.), 77; *Fairchild* v. *Bascomb*, 35 Vt. 398.
(*q*) *Re Toomes*, 54 Cal. 575.
(*r*) Greenleaf's Evidence, 12th Ed., I. p. 483; *Livingstone's case*, 14 Grat. 592.
(*s*) *Lorg* v. *First German Congregation*, 63 Pa. St. 156; *Hills* v. *Home Ins. Co.*, 129 Mass., 544, 551.
(*t*) *Lester* v. *Pittsford*, 7 Vt. 161; *Mendum* v. *Com.* 6 Rand. 704; *Tullis* v. *Kidd*, 12 Ala. 648; *Sinclair* v. *Rourk*, 14 Ind. 540; *Winans* v. *N. Y., etc., R. R. Co.*, 21 How. (U. S.) 88; *Boardman* v. *Woodman*, 47 N. H. 121; *Davis* v. *State*, 35 Ind. 496.

"We find no test laid down," says the Supreme Court of Indiana, "by which we can determine with mathematical precision just how much experience a witness must have had, how expert, in short, he must be, to render him competent to testify as an expert." But it is for the Court to decide, within the limits of a fair discretion, whether the experience of the proposed expert has been such as to make his opinions of any value; mere opportunities for special observation will not be deemed sufficient (*u*).

While the Court, or Judge, determines the competency of the witness to testify as an expert, the weight to be accorded to his testimony is for the jury to decide. The testimony of an expert is to be weighed and tested like any other kind of evidence, and is to receive just such credit as the jury may think it entitled to. It is intended to enlighten their minds, not control their judgment (*v*). The jury are not bound by the opinions of medical experts: they may weigh their opinions like any other evidence. They may act against the greater number of opinions and in favour of the fewer; for the opinion of one expert may, on account of his greater knowledge and experience on the subject, or from his giving further details of the case, or more probable reasons for his opinions, be of greater value to the jury than the opposite opinions of several (*w*).

Ordronaux holds that a physician, although confessedly possessing the ordinary experience of his profession, may *quoad* some particular problem in medical science not be an expert in the best and most critical sense of the term. *Non omnes omnia possumus.* Once received as an expert,

---

(*u*) *Forgery* v. *First Nat. Bank,* 66 Ind. 123, 125; *McEwen* v. *Bigelow,* 40 Mich. 217; *Kilborne* v. *Jennings,* 38 Iowa, 533.

(*v*) *Mitchell* v. *State,* 58 Ala 418; *Forgery* v. *First Nat. Bank,* 66 Ind. 123; *Parnell* v. *Commonwealth,* 86 Pa. St. 269; *Carter* v. *Baker,* 1 Sawy. (U. S. C. C.) 525.

(*w*) *Tatum* v. *Mohr,* 21 Ark. 355; *Getchell* v. *Hill,* 21 Minn. 464.

the maxim "*Cuilibet in sua arte perito credendum est,*" must be applied, and he cannot be contradicted by any unskilled person (*x*).

In 1869, the Chief Justice of the Kentucky Court of Appeal well said, that "the opinion of experts not founded on science, but on a mere theory of morals or ethics, whether given by professional or unprofessional men, are wholly inadmissible as evidence. Hence the opinion of even physicians that no sane man in a Christian country would commit suicide, not being founded on the science or phenomena of the mind, but rather a theory of morals, religion and future responsibility, is not evidence (*y*).

In the matter of expert testimony, as in other matters, the law does not recognize any particular school of medicine to the exclusion of others. The popular axiom that doctors differ is as true now as ever it was, and so long as it continues to be so, it is impossible for the law to recognize any class of practitioners, or the followers of any particular system, or method of treatment, as exclusively entitled to be regarded as "doctors" (*z*).

The physician called to give evidence as an expert should understand at the outset that he is not called to express any opinion upon the merits of the case, but only on some questions of science raised by the facts proved; that he has no concern in the issue of the trial, and that whichever side calls him he is in no wise the witness—much less the advocate—of that side. He is truly an adviser of the Court, an *amicus curiæ*, rather than a party interested in the result of the trial. Balbus in his commentaries on the code says, "*Medici proprie non sunt testes, sed est magis judicium quam testimonium.*" Experts, no matter on what

---

(*x*) Ordronaux Principles, sec. 108-110.
(*y*) *St. Louis Mut. Ins. Co.* v. *Graves*, 6 Bush. 290.
(*z*) *Corsi* v. *Maretzek*, 4 E. D. Smith, 1.

they testify, simply supply data, as to whose competency, relevancy and weight, the Court is to judge, and as to which the Court is finally to declare the law. Where the facts testified to by experts are undisputed, and when they are the results of a particular science or art, with which such experts are familiar, then the Court accepts such facts, and declares the law that therefrom springs; where the facts are disputed then the jury is to determine where the preponderance of proof lies. But when the testimony of the expert touches either law or speculation, psychology or ethics, then such testimony is to be received as mere argument, which if admissible at all is to be treated simply as if addressed to the judgment of the Court (a).

In his examination in chief an expert may not only give his opinion itself, but also the grounds and reasons of it; in fact it has been held that it is his duty to state the reasons of his opinion and the facts on which it is based, and if it is not sustained by them it is entitled to little weight (b).

The opinion of a medical man is admissible upon, the condition of the human system at any given time; the nature and symptoms of disease; the nature and effects of wounds; the cause of death; the cause or effect of an injury; the character of the instrument with which a wound was produced; the effect of a particular course of treatment; the likelihood of recovery; the mental condition of a person; and on similar subjects. For instance, where one was indicted for endeavouring to procure abortion, the opinion that the woman was pregnant at the time is relevant (c). Where the question was whether a certain

---

(a) Wharton on Mental Unsoundness sec. 282.
(b) *Keith* v. *Lothrop*, 10 Cush. 453; *Clark* v. *State*, 12 Ohio, 483.
(c) Rules Relating to Opinion Evidence, 26 A. L. J. 486; *State* v. *Smith*, 32 Me. 370; *Young* v. *Makepeace*, 103 Mass. 50.

blow was sufficient to cause death; or whether a wound and fracture on the head was caused by a fall; or whether the fractures of the skull were caused by a gun; or whether a gun-shot wound caused death; the opinions of physicians were held admissible (*d*). The opinion of medical experts will be received upon the question as to whether an abortion has been performed, or whether certain drugs are abortives, or certain instruments adapted to produce an abortion (*e*). Experts may testify, after having made a chemical analysis of the contents of the stomach, as to the presence of poison in the body; and, without such analysis of a mixture, a chemist may speak of its ingredients (*f*). Those accustomed to make chemical and microscopic examinations of blood and blood stains may speak as to whether certain stains are made by human or other blood. So, too, they may speak as to the ink in questions as to handwriting (*g*). So, too, they may be asked their opinions touching the permanency of any injury forming the subject of an action. Also, in an action for damages against a railway company, a physician may be asked at what period after the injury the plaintiff would be most likely to improve, if he were going to recover at all (*h*). Where Barber sued Meriam for injury to his wife, and she had been treated professionally for some weeks by Dr. H., the opinion of another physician as to the effect of Dr. H.'s treatment was considered

---

(*d*) *State* v. *Powell*, 7 N. J. (L.), 269; *Davis* v. *State*, 38 Ind. 37; *Gardner* v. *People*, 6 Parker, C. C. 202; overruling, *Wilson* v. *People*, 4 Park., C. C. 619; *State* v. *Jones*, 68 N. C. 443.

(*e*) *State* v. *Smith*, Supra; *Regina* v. *Stitt*, 30 U. C. C. P. 30; *State* v. *Wood*, 53 N. H. 484.

(*f*) *State* v. *Bowman*, 78 N. C. 509; *State* v. *Slagh*, 83 N. C. 630.

(*g*) *Com.* v. *Sturtevant*, 117 Mass. 122.

(*h*) *Newell* v. *Doty*, 33 N. Y. 83; *Buell* v. *N. Y. C.*, 31 N. Y. Ct. of App. 314; *Matteson* v. *N. Y. C.* 62 Barb. 366; S. C. 35 N. Y. 487.

(*i*) 11 Allen, 322.

(*j*) *R.* v. *Whitehead*, 3 C. & K. 203; *Rich* v. *Pierpont*, 3 F. & F. 36; *Twombly* v. *Leach*, 11 Cush. 405..

admissible (*i*). And so in a case of malpractice a medical man may be asked whether the practice pursued was good practice (*j*). He may be asked as to the nature and and properties of the medicines employed by another physician in the case in question; also, as to the practice with regard to consultations; also, whether, in his opinion, a patient's death was or was not the result of neglect or want of skill on the part of the attending physician (*k*). But he cannot be asked his opinion as to the general skill of the physician on trial; nor the general reputation of the school which the doctor in trouble attended; nor can he say whether, from all the evidence in the case, the defendant was guilty of malpractice, for that is the question for the jury; nor can he say whether a physician has honorably and faithfully discharged his duty to his professional brethren (*l*).

It has been held that a medical witness may give his opinion upon new and hitherto unknown cases whenever he swears that he can form such an opinion, even though at the same time he should admit that precisely such a case had never before fallen under his observation, nor under his notice in the books. The man of science is distinguished from the empiric in nothing more than in not relying on specifics, and also not waiting for the exact similitudes in things material and immaterial before forming a judgment as to their similarity (*m*).

It must always be remembered that medical men, when called as skilled witnesses, may only say what, in their judgment, would be the result of certain facts submitted to their consideration, and may not give an opinion as to

---

(*k*) *Mertz* v. *Detweeler*, 8 W. & S. 376; *Wright* v. *Hardy*, 22 Wisc. 368.

(*l*) *Leighton* v. *Sargent*, 11 Fost. N. H. 120; *Williams* v. *Poppleton*, 3 Oregon, 139; *Hoener* v. *Koch*, 84 Ill. 408; *Ramadge* v. *Ryan*, 9 Bing. 333.

(*m*) *State* v. *Clark*, 12 Ired. 151; *Page* v. *Barker*, 40 N. H. 477.

the general merits of the case, nor on the very point which the jury has to determine, nor on things with which a jury may be supposed to be equally well acquainted (*n*).

As a recent writer puts it, a medical man cannot testify as to matters not of skill in his profession, nor conclusions, nor inferences which it is the duty of the jury to draw for themselves. For instance, it was held that in a trial for murder the opinions of the surgeons as to the probable position of the deceased, when he received the blows which caused his death, are incompetent. The Judge said that he was not aware that surgeons were experts in the manner of giving blows of the description in question, or determining how the head must be placed so as most conveniently to receive them (*o*). Whenever the subject matter of the enquiry is of such a character that it may be presumed to lie within the common experience of all men of common education, moving in ordinary walks of life, the rule is that the opinions of experts are inadmissible, as the jury are supposed—in all such matters—to be entirely competent to draw the necessary inferences from the facts spoken of by the witnesses (*p*). Nor was the opinion of a medical witness admitted where the question, in an action for libel, was whether a physician in refusing to consult with the plaintiff had honorably and faithfully discharged his duty to the medical profession. The Judge said, the jury having all the facts before them were as capable of forming a judgment upon that point as the witness himself. Nor can an expert give an opinion of the opinion on another expert (*q*). A medical man is considered an expert on the subject of the

---

(*n*) *Ramadge* v. *Ryan*, 9 Bing. 335; *R.* v. *Searle*, 1 M. & Rob. 75; *Fenwick* v. *Bell*, 1 C. & Kir. 312; *Gibson* v. *Williams*, 4 Wend. 320; *Morse* v. *State*, 6 Conn. 9.

(*o*) *Kennedy* v. *People*, 39 N. Y. 245.

(*p*) *New England Glass Co.* v. *Lovell*, 7 Cush. 319.

(*q*) *Ramadge* v. *Ryan*, supra; *Campbell* v. *Richards*, 5 B. & Ad. 840.

value of medical services (*r*). But he is not so considered when the question is one as to the amount of damages for a breach of contract not to practise physic in a certain town (*s*).

The rule as to excluding experts from the court room during the examination of witnesses has been laid down, in England, thus: " Medical or other professional witnesses, who are summoned to give scientific opinions upon the circumstances of the case, as established by other testimony, will be permitted to remain in court until this particular class of evidence commences; but then, like ordinary witnesses, they will have to withdraw, and to come in one by one, so as to undergo a separate examination." And in the United States the principle is similarly stated (*t*).

(*r*) *Reynolds* v. *Robinson*, 64 N. Y. 595; *Shafer* v. *Deans ad'mor*, 29 Ia. 144.
(*s*) *Linn* v. *Sigsbee*, 67 Ill. 75; see *Bradbury* v. *Barden*, 35 Conn. 580.
(*t*) 2 Taylor's Evid., sec. 1259; 1 Wharton's Evid., sec. 492.

# CHAPTER IX.

### EXPERTS IN INSANITY CASES.

The opinion evidence of medical men in questions of insanity is not, as a rule, looked upon with any very great degree of favor by the courts who have to decide upon the competency, relevancy and weight of the opinions uttered. Chapman, C.J., of Massachusetts, in charging a jury said, "While they afford great aid in determining facts, it often happens that experts can be found to testify to anything however absurd" (a). In another insanity case another Judge remarked, "Experience has shown that opposite opinions of persons professing to be experts may be obtained to any amount, and it often occurs that not only many days but many weeks are consumed in cross-examinations to test the skill and knowledge of such witnesses, and to test the correctness of their opinions," (this was the case to a great degree in the well known Guiteau prosecution,) "thus wasting time and wearying the patience of both Court and jury, perplexing, instead of elucidating, the question involved in the issue" (b). As to the perplexing instead of elucidating, a writer of the highest authority gives the following, "In a case of alleged child murder a medical witness, being asked for a plain opinion of the cause of death, said, that it was owing to "atelectasis and a general engorgement of the pulmonary tissue." And in a trial for an assault a

---

(a) Bost. Med. and Sur. Journ., Feb. 25, 1869.
(b) Grier, J., in *Winans* v. *N. Y. & E. R.* 21 How. (U. S.) 88.

surgeon, in giving his evidence, informed the Court "that on examining the prosecutor, he found him suffering from a severe contusion of the integument under the left orbit, with great extravasation of blood and ecchymosis in the surrounding cellular tissue, which was in a tumefied state, and there was also considerable abrasion of the cuticle." The Judge said, "You mean, I suppose, that the man had a bad black eye." "Yes." "Then why not say so at once" (c).

Redfield, C.J., in his book on Wills, says, "Experience has shown both here and in England that medical experts differ quite as widely in their inferences and opinions as do other witnesses. This has become so uniform a result with the medical experts of late that they are beginning to be regarded much in the light of hired advocates, and their testimony as nothing more than a studied argument in favor of the side for which they have been called. So uniformly has this been proved in our experience that it would excite scarcely less surprise to find an expert called on one side testifying in any particular in favor of the other side, than to find the counsel upon either side arguing against their clients and in favor of their antagonists" (d).

A Lord Chancellor once remarked that his experience taught him that there were very few cases of insanity in which any good came from the examination of medical men. Their evidence sometimes adorned a case, and gave rise to very agreeable and interesting scientific discussions, but after all they have little or no weight with the jury. And Mr. Justice Davis, of the Supreme Court of Maine, after stating that he thought juries far more trust-worthy than experts on the subject of insanity, said, "if there is any kind of testimony that is not only of no value but

(c) Taylor's Med. Jur. 6 Am. Ed. 53.
(d) Vol. i. p. 103.

even worse than that, it is in my judgment that of medical experts. They may be able to state the diagnosis of the disease more learnedly, but upon the question whether it had, at a given time, reached such a stage that the subject of it was incapable of making a contract, or irresponsible for his acts, the opinion of his neighbors, if men of good common sense, would be worth more than that of all the experts in the country" (*e*). There is scarcely a single hypothesis as to responsibility (on the part of the insane), no matter how wild, which, among the large number of experts who have concerned themselves with this branch of study, has not its advocates. So says Wharton in his valuable treatise on Mental Unsoundness (*f*); or as Cicero elegantly put it long ago, "*nihil tam absurde dici potest, quod non dicatur ab aliquo philosophorum*" (*g*).

Considering these things, one is not surprised at Campbell, C.J., in the Bambridge case, saying to three medical men who had recorded their opinions in favor of the insanity of the testator: "You may go home to your patients, and I wish you may be more usefully employed there, than you have been here;" and to the jury he remarked, "We have had during the trial the evidence of three medical witnesses, and I think they might as well have stayed at home and attended to their patients."

On the other hand, Shaw, C.J., said, "such opinions (as to sanity, etc.) when they come from persons of experience, and in whose correctness and sobriety of judgment just confidence can be had, are of great weight, and deserve the respectful consideration of a jury. But the opinion of a medical man of small experience, or of one who has crude and visionary notions, or who has some favorite theory to

---

(*e*) Redfield on Wills, vol. i. cap. 3, sec. 13.
(*f*) Sec. 195.
(*g*) De Divinatione, II. 58.

support is entitled to very little consideration. The value of such testimony will depend mainly upon the experience, fidelity and impartiality of the witness who gives it " (*h*). And Chief Justice Gibson speaks with just emphasis of the the deference due, in their own department, to the knowledge obtained by men of a subject with which they have grappled all their lives (*i*). The Supreme Court of Texas declared, "The opinions of medical men (on questions of insanity) are received with great respect and consideration, and properly so." The Supreme Court of Pennsylvania says, "It is well settled that the knowledge and experience of medical experts is of great value in questions of insanity." Equally strong are the utterances of the Court of Appeals of West Virginia and the Supreme Court of North Carolina (*j*).

Where the point in question is the sanity of a person, the opinion of a medical man on the subject is, of course, admissible when that opinion is drawn from personal observation. This is the rule both in England and the United States (*k*). But a medical man may also give his opinion on this subject, even though he has no knowledge of the person whose sanity is in question (*l*). It has been suggested, that when a physician is asked his opinion on the facts stated by other witnesses, he should be first examined as to the particular symptoms of insanity; and as to whether all or any, and which of the circumstances spoken of by the witnesses upon the trial are to be regarded as

---

(*h*) *Com. v. Rodgers*, 7 Metc. 5.

(*i*) Wharton on Mental Unsoundness, sec. 293.

(*j*) *Thomas v. State*, 40 Texas, 65; *Parmell v. Com.*, 86 Pa. St. 260; *Jarrett v. Jarrett*, 11 W. Va. 627; *Flynt v. Bodenhamer*, 80 N. C. 205.

(*k*) *Rex v. Searle*, 1 Mood. & Rob. 75; *R. v. Offord*, 5 C. & P. 168; *McAllister v. State*, 17 Ala. 434; *Delafield v. Parish*, 25 N. Y. 9; *Com. v. Rodgers*, 7 Metc. 5; *Clark v. State*, 12 Oh. 483; *Davis v. State*, 35 Ind. 496.

(*l*) *Puryear v. Reese*, 46 Tenn. 21; *White v. Bailey*, 10 Mich. 155; *Dickenson v. Barber*, 9 Mass. 225.

such symptoms; then inquire of him whether any and what combination of these circumstances would, in his opinion, amount to proof of insanity (*m*).

It has been held to be improper to ask a medical witness whether the person, whose sanity was in question, possessed sufficient capacity to make a will, or to transact business, as these are matters of law, depending on the nature of the business (*n*). In England such witnesses can only speak as to the state of mind, not as to the responsibility of a prisoner; this latter point is for the jury under the direction of the Judge (*o*). So, on the plea of insanity at the time of making a contract, the opinion of the medical man who gave the certificate on which the defendant was confined as insane at or about the time, is only evidence for the jury, who must judge of the grounds upon which it was formed (*p*).

In England, an expert cannot be asked, after being present at the whole trial, whether the defendant was insane, or whether the act complained of was an insane act, because these are questions for the jury and the witness must not be placed in the jury's place; but he may be asked whether such and such appearances, proved by other witnesses, are in his judgment symptoms of insanity (*q*). The particular facts proven by other witnesses may be taken and the expert may be asked "assuming these facts to be true, do they in your judgment indicate insanity on the part of the defendant at the time the alleged act was committed?" (*r*).

(*m*) *People* v. *McGann*, 3 Parker Cr. Cas. 272, 298.
(*n*) *White* v. *Bailey*, 10 Mich. 155; *Fairfield* v. *Bascomb*, 35 Vt. 398.
(*o*) *R.* v. *Richards*, 1 F. & F. 87.
(*p*) *Lovatt* v. *Tribe*, 3 F. & F. 9.
(*q*) *R.* v. *Higginson*, 1 Car. & R. 129; *R.* v. *Searle*, 1 Mood. & Rob. 75; *Malton* v. *Nesbit*, 1 C. & P. 72; *R.* v. *Wright*, Russ. & Ry. 456; see, also, *Tingley* v. *Cougill*, 48 Mo. 297.
(*r*) *R.* v. *Frances*, 4 Cox C. C. 57; *R.* v. *Searle*, sup.

As a rule the Court should not allow an expert to give his opinion upon facts proved by a witness unless he has heard all the testimony of the witness, because the entire testimony may be necessary in order to enable him to form an opinion in regard to the subject matter of inquiry (*s*).

Where the facts are disputed, experts can only be questioned as to their opinion of a party's sanity on a hypothetical case, or as to certain designated facts existing in the case supposing them to be true (*t*).

The mode in which this hypothetical question is to be put has been much considered. In England, in the celebrated *Macnaghten* case in answer to an inquiry of the House of Lords, whether "a medical man conversant with the disease of insanity, who never saw the prisoner previously to the trial, but who was present during the whole trial and the examination of the witnesses, can be asked his opinion as to the state of the prisoner's mind at the time of the commission of the alleged crime; or his opinion whether the prisoner was conscious at the time of doing the act, that he was acting contrary to the law; or whether he was labouring under any and what delusion at the time?" The twelve judges replied, "We think the medical man, under the circumstances supposed, cannot in strictness be asked his opinion in the terms above stated, because each of these questions involves the determination of the facts deposed to, which it is for the jury to decide, and the questions are not mere questions upon a matter of science in which case such evidence is admissible. But where the facts are admitted or not disputed, and the question becomes substantially one of science only, it may be convenient to

---

(*s*) *Page* v. *State*, 61 Ala. 18; *Davis* v. *State*, 38 Md. 41.

(*t*) *Fairchild* v. *Bascomb*, 35 Vt. 398; *State* v. *Windsor*, 5 Harring. 512; *U. S.* v. *McGlue*, 1 Curtis C. C. 1; *McAlister* v. *State*, 17 Ala. 434; *Woodbury* v. *Obear*, 7 Gray, 467; *Hunt* v. *Lowell Gas Light Company*, 8 Allan, 169.

allow the question to be put in that general form, though the same cannot be insisted on as a matter of right (*u*).

In Massachusetts, Chief Justice Shaw said, "The proper question to be put to the professional witness is this—If the symptoms and indications testified to by the other witnesses are proved and if the jury are satisfied of the truth of them, whether in their opinion the party was insane, and what was the nature and character of that insanity; what state of mind did they indicate; and what they would expect would be the conduct of such person in any supposed circumstances?" (*v*).

In another well known case, the Judge said to the jury, "It is not the province of the expert to draw inferences of facts from the evidence, but simply to declare his opinion on a known, or hypothetical state of facts, and therefore the counsel on each side have put to the physicians such states of fact as they deem warranted by the evidence, and have taken their opinions thereon. If you consider any of these states of facts put to the medical witnesses are proved, then the opinions thereon are admissible evidence, to be weighed by you, otherwise their opinions are not applicable to the case" (*w*).

The opinions of both experts and non-experts should have weight according to their opportunities and qualifications for examination of the state of mind of the person whose sanity is in question. First of all will be the family, or the physician who has attended the patient through the disease which is supposed to have disabled his mind; next are those who, without special learning on the subject, have had the best opportunities for judging—the members of his family and those whose intimacy in the family, have given them opportunities of seeing the patient at all times and

(*u*) 10 Clark & Fin. 200.
(*v*) *Com.* v. *Rodgers,* 7 Metc. 5.
(*w*) *U. S.* v. *McGlue,* 1 Cur. C. C. 1.

noticing the alienation of his mind; and last, come those who only occasionally and at intervals have seen him, and whose chances of studying his moods have been small (*x*).

It has been held, in Massachusetts, that a physician who had not made insanity a special subject, and who, when consulted in such matters, always called in a specialist, is not competent to give an opinion on an hypothetical case put to him, unless he was the person's attending physician; then his opinion is received, as it is his duty to make himself acquainted with the peculiarities, bodily and mental, of a person who is the subject of his care and advice (*y*). And where a physician had for more than thirty years been exclusively treating the insane, he was not permitted to testify, as an expert, to the mental capacity of a person—not previously insane—who was in the last stages of disease (*z*).

One not an expert may give an opinion, founded on observation, as to whether a person is sane or insane, notwithstanding the general rule, that persons not medical men cannot give their opinions as to the existence, nature or extent of disease in any one. The exception was first introduced in regard to the subscribing witnesses to a will, who were permitted to speak as to the testator's state of mind; it has now been extended to all cases where the witness' acquaintance with the party whose sanity is in dispute, or his means of observation, are sufficient to enable him to express his opinion as to the mental condition. The Courts of Massachussetts, Maine, New Hampshire and Texas, however, still adhere to the old rule and admit the evidence of non-experts only in cases of wills (*a*).

(*x*) *Burton* v. *Scott*, 3 Rand. 399; 27 A. L. J. 148.
(*y*) *Com.* v. *Rich*, 14 Gray, 335; *Hastings* v. *Rider*, 99 Mass. 625; *Russell* v. *State*, 53 Miss. 36.
(*z*) *Heald* v. *Wing*, 5 Me. 392; *Whetherbee* v. *Whetherbee*, 38 Vt. 454.
(*a*) 27 Alb. L. J. 126.

## CHAPTER X.

### DEFAMATION.

No man may disparage the reputation of another. Every one has a right to have his good name maintained, unimpaired. Words which produce any perceptible injury to the reputation of another are called defamatory : and if they are false they are actionable. False and malicious defamatory words, if in printing, writing, pictures or signs, and published, constitute a libel; if spoken, a slander. A caricature may be a libel; so may a chalk-mark on a wall, a statue, hieroglyphics, a rebus, an anagram or an allegory, or even ironical praise.

Defamatory matter, whether published in the form of libel or slander, is actionable when it imputes a criminal offence (or a contagious or infectious disorder) or affects the plaintiff injuriously in his lawful profession, trade or business, or in the discharge of a public office, or generally when it is false and malicious, and its publication causes damage to the plaintiff either in law or in fact. Defamatory matter, the publication of which tends to degrade or disparage the plaintiff, or which renders him ridiculous, or charges him with want of honesty, humanity or veracity, or is intended to impair his enjoyment of society, fortune or comfort, is actionable as libel, but not as slander, unless special damage be proved (a).

(a) Glenn's Laws of Med. Men, p. 212.

The person defamed by a libel has not only a civil remedy to recover damages but he may also, in some cases, proceed criminally by way of information or indictment and have the defamer punished as an offender against the state. If he proceeds by information he must in general waive his right to bring a civil action; but he may sue for damages after the offender has been convicted upon an indictment. An action for libel must be brought within six years; and an action for slander within two years, unless the words spoken are actionable only by reason of special damage, in which case the action may be brought at any time within six years.

Whenever a special kind of knowledge is essential to the proper conduct of a particular profession, denying that a man possesses such special knowledge will be actionable if he belongs to that particular profession, but not otherwise. Thus to say of a physican, "Thou art a drunken fool and an ass. Thou wert never a scholar, nor even able to speak like a scholar," is actionable, because no man can be a good physician unless he be a scholar (b). Although one may with impunity say of a Justice of the Peace, "He is a fool, an ass and a beetle headed justice" (c). So to say, of a midwife, "Many have perished for her want of skill;" or, "She is an ignorant woman, and of small practice and very unfortunate in her way; there are few she goes to but lie desperately ill, or die under her hands;" is actionable (d). Or of an apothecary, "He is not an apothecary; he has not passed any examination. Several have died that he had attended, and there have been inquests held upon them" (e). Although one may safely say of a Justice of the Peace, "He is a blood sucker, and sucketh blood."

(b) *Cawdry* v. *Highley*, Cro. Car. 270 ; Godb. 441.
(c) *Bill* v. *Neal*, 1 Sev. 52.
(d) *Flower's* Case, Cro. Car. 211; *Wharton* v. *Brook*, Vent. 21.
(e) *Southee* v. *Denny*, 1 Ex. 196.

It is actionable to say of a person in his professional character, "He is no doctor; he bought his diploma for $50" (*f*). Any words imputing to a practising medical man, misconduct or incapacity in the discharge of his professional duties, are actionable *per se*. Thus, it is actionable, without proof of special damage, to accuse one of having caused the death of any patient through his ignorance or culpable negligence, as to say of a physician, "He killed my child by giving it too much calomel," or, "He hath killed J. S. with physic, which physic was a pill;" or, "He was the death of J. P.; he has killed his patient with physic; it is a world of blood he has to answer for in this town through his ignorance; he did kill a woman and two children at Southampton; he did kill J. P. at Petersfield;" or, as an American did, "Dr. S. killed my children; he gave them teaspoonful doses of calomel, and it killed them. They did not live long after they took it. They died right off the same day" (*g*).

So it is to say of an apothecary, "He poisoned my uncle; I will have him digged up again, and hang him," or, "He killed my child; it was the saline injection that did it;" or, "I was told he had given my child too much mercury, and poisoned it; otherwise, it would have got well" (*h*).

So it is actionable to say of a surgeon and accoucheur, "He is a bad character; none of the medical men here will meet him." As such words impart the want of a necessary qualification for a surgeon in the ordinary discharge of his professional duties; or, "Dr. Tweedie has honorably and faithfully discharged his duties to his medi-

(*f*) *Bergold* v. *Puckta*, 2 Thomp. & C. N. Y. 532.
(*g*) *Johnson* v. *Robertson*, 8 Port. R. 586; *Poe* v. *Mondford*, Cro. Eliz. 620; *Tutty* v. *Alewin*, 11 Mod. 221; *Secord* v. *Harris*, 18 Barb. 425; see, also, *Watson* v. *Vanderlash*, Het. 69.
(*h*) *Davis* v. *Ockham*, Sty. 235; *Edsall* v. *Russell*, 4 M. & G. 1090.

cal brethren in refusing to act or consult with Ramadge (a physician), and we hope every one else will do the same" (*i*). Or to call a practising medical man " a quack," " a quacksalver," " an empiric," or " a mountebank," or to say of him, " Thou gavest physic which thou knewest to be contrary to the disease," or " Thou art no good subject, for thou poisonedst A. F.'s wound, to get more money of him." Under the New York Statutes, a homœopathic physician may maintain an action for being called a quack (*j*). And it seems that an action will lie, without averment of special damages, for slander imputing to a physician, that he has taken advantage of his character as a physician to abuse the confidence reposed in him, and commit acts of criminal conversation with a patient (*k*).

In the case of libel, any words will be presumed defamatory which expose the plaintiff to hatred, contempt, ridicule or obloquy, which tend to injure him in his professional trade, or cause him to be shunned or avoided by his neighbours. Thus, to advertise falsely that certain quack medicines, " consumption pills," were prepared by a physician of eminence, is a libel upon such physician (*l*).

Whenever a medical man brings forward some new method of treatment and advertises it largely as the best, or only cure for some particular disease, or for all diseases at once, he may be said to invite public attention, and a newspaper writer is justified in warning the public against such advertisers, and in exposing the absurdity of their professions, provided he does so fairly and with reasonable judgment (*m*).

(*i*) *Southee* v. *Denny*, 1 Ex. 196; *Ramadge* v. *Ryan*, 9 Bing. 333.

(*j*) *Long* v. *Chubb*, 5 C. & P. 55; *Allen* v. *Eaton*, 1 Roll. Abr. 54; *Goddart* v. *Haselfoot*, 1 Viner's Abr. (S. A.) pl. 12; *White* v. *Carroll*, 42 N. Y. 161.

(*k*) *Ayre* v. *Craven*, 2 Ad. & E. 2.

(*l*) *Clarke* v. *Freeman*, 11 Beav. 112; *Ramadge* v. *Wakley*, cited 9 Bing. 333.

(*m*) Odgers on Libel and Slander, p. 50.

A medical man, who had obtained a diploma and the degree of M.D., from an American College, advertised in England most extensively a new and infallible cure for consumption. The *Pall Mall Gazette* published a leading article on these advertisements, in which they called the advertiser a quack and an impostor, and compared him to scoundrels "who pass bad coin." This was considered as overstepping the limits of fair criticism, and a verdict was given for the plaintiff, with damages, one farthing (*n*). So where the editor of the *Lancet* attacked the editor of a rival paper, *The London Medical and Physical Journal*, by rancorous aspersions on his private character, not fairly called for by what the plaintiff had done as an editor, the plaintiff recovered a verdict of £5 (*o*).

On the other hand, it is not actionable to say of a surgeon, "He did poison the wound of his patient," without some averment that this was improper treatment, for it might be proper for the cure of it. Nor to say of an apothecary, "He made up the medicine for my child wrong, through jealousy, because I would not allow him to use his own judgment" (*p*). Nor to charge a physician or surgeon with "malpractice," if it appear that the word was not used or understood in a technical sense; and to charge a physician or surgeon with mere want of skill, or with ignorance or neglect, is not actionable *per se*, though untrue, unless the charge be of gross want of skill, or the like, so as to imply general unfitness (*q*).

Nor is it actionable to call a person who practises medicine or surgery, without legal qualification, a "quack or an

---

(*n*) *Hunter* v. *Sharpe*, 4 F. & F. 983; and see *Morrison* v. *Harmer*, 4 Scott, 524.

(*o*) *Macleod* v. *Wakley*, 3 C. & P. 311.

(*p*) *Sugoe's* Case, Hetl. 175; *Edsall* v. *Russell*, 4 M. & G. 1090.

(*q*) *Rodgers* v. *Cline*, 56 Miss. 808; *Camp* v. *Martin*, 23 Conn. 86; *Jones* v. *Diver*, 22 Ind. 184.

impostor," for the law only protects lawful employment (r). Even though a medical man be duly registered in Great Britain, still, if he is practising in a colony which requires registration without complying with the colonial law, he may safely be called "a quack," "a charlatan," "a scoundrel not to be entrusted with the lives of people" (s).

Words imputing immoral conduct, profligacy or adultery, even when spoken of one holding an office or carrying on a profession or business, are not actionable unless they "touch him" in that office, profession or business. Thus, if adultery is alleged of a clergyman, it will be actionable, because if the charge were true, it would be a ground for degradation or deprivation, as it would prove him unfit to hold his benefice, or to continue the active duties of his profession. But if the same words are spoken of a physician, they will not be actionable without proof of special damage, as they do not necessarily affect the plaintiff in relation to his trade or profession (t).

Nor unless the words are spoken in connection with the professional duties of the plaintiff will an action lie for the words, "He is so steady drunk, he cannot get business any more;" or "He is a twopenny bleeder" (u).

It is no libel to write of a physician that he is in the habit of meeting homœopathists in consultation (v).

Where the plaintiff considers that the words spoken touch him in his profession or trade, he must always aver in the pleadings that he was carrying on the profession of a physician or surgeon, or the trade of a druggist, at the

(r) *Collins* v. *Carnegie*, 1 A. & E. 695.
(s) *Skirving* v. *Ross*, 31 C. P. (Ont.) 423.
(t) *Ayre* v. *Craven*, 2 A. & E. 2; *Dixon* v. *Smith*, 5 H. & N. 450.
(u) *Anon.* 1 Ham. 83; *Foster* v. *Small*, 3 Whart. 138.
(v) *Clay* v. *Roberts*, 9 Jur. (N. S.) 580).

time the words were spoken. Sometimes this is admitted by the slander itself, and if so, evidence is of course unnecessary in proof of this averment. But in other cases, unless it is admitted on the pleadings, evidence must be given at the trial of the special character in which the plaintiff sues. As a rule, it is sufficient for the plaintiff to prove that he was engaged in the profession or trade, without proving any appointment thereto, or producing a diploma or other formal qualification. For the maxim *omnia presumuntur rite esse acta* applies. But if the very slander complained of imputes to the medical practitioner that he is a quack or an impostor, not legally qualified for practice; or if the plaintiff aver that he is a physician and has duly taken his degree, then the plaintiff at the trial must be prepared to prove his qualification strictly by producing his diploma or certificate. In some cases the mere production of the diploma will not be sufficient proof of the plaintiff's having the degree, but it may be necessary to prove that the seal affixed is the seal of a university having power to grant degrees; or in the case of the production of a copy of the diploma, that it has been compared with the original (*w*).

Whether or no the words were spoken of the plaintiff in the way of his business is a question for the jury to determine at the trial. There should always be an averment in the statement of claim, that the words were so spoken, and it should also be shewn in what manner the words were connected by the speaker with the profession (*x*).

Medical practitioners are of course equally liable with other men to an action for defamation, in respect of any

---

(*w*) Odgers on Slander, p. 69; *Rutherford* v. *Evans*, 4 C. & P. 79; *Collins* v. *Carnegie*, 1 Ad. & E. 697; *Moises* v. *Thornton*, 3 Esp. 4; *Wakley* v. *Healey*, 4 Ex. 53.

(*x*) *Van Tassel* v. *Capson*, 1 Denio. 250; *Kinney* v. *Nash*, 3 Comst. 177; *Ayre* v. *Craven*, sup.

false and malicious communication, whether oral or written, made by them to the damage of another, in law or in fact; circumstances, however, frequently arise where, from the nature of their employment, it becomes their duty or interest to make some communication prejudicial to the character or conduct of another, and in such cases, where the occasion on which the communication was made rebuts the presumption of malice,(which the law infers from such a statement,) such communication is said to be privileged, and therefore, in order to sustain an action for defamation, the plaintiff must prove that the defendant was actuated by express or actual malice—that is, malice independent of the occasion on which the communication was made. The legal canon is, that a communication made *bona fide*, upon any subject matter in which the party communicating has an interest, or in reference to which he has a duty, is privileged, if made to a person having a corresponding interest or duty, although it contains criminatory matter, which (without this privilege) would be slanderous and actionable. This applies, moreover, though the duty be not a legal one, but only a moral or social duty of imperfect obligation, and also where the communication is made to a person not in fact having such interest or duty, but who might reasonably be, and is supposed by the party making the communication to have such interest or duty (*y*). Even where the evidence of duty is not present to the mind, but the speaker is impelled by a sense of propriety, on which he does not pause to reflect, and which he refers to no special motive, nevertheless, if his conduct in speaking the words be within the occasion of interest or of duty which is capable of protecting, the communication will be considered privileged (*z*).

Words spoken by the medical officer of a college concerning

(*y*) Glenn's Laws of Med. Men, 230; *Harrison* v. *Bush*, 5 El. & B. 344.
(*z*) Per Pigot, C.B., in *Bell* v. *Parke*, 10 Ir. C. L. Rep., N. S., 288.

the meat furnished to the institution; and words used by the medical attendant of a poor-law union about the wine supplied to the inmates, are privileged, in the absence of proof of actual malice (*a*). A statement made by a physician that an unmarried woman is pregnant is not a privileged communication, unless made in good faith to one who is reasonably entitled to receive the information (*b*).

(*a*) *Humphreys* v. *Stilwell*, 2 F. & F. 590; *Murphey* v. *Kellett*, 13 Ir. C. L. Rep. N. S. 638.
(*b*) *Alpen* v. *Morton*, 21 Oh. St. 536.

## CHAPTER XI.

### RELATIONS WITH PATIENTS.

It is a well settled doctrine that where one occupying a position which naturally gives him the confidence of another, or which in any way gives him an influence, or an undue advantage over the other, transactions between them require something more to give them validity than is necessary in other cases. The mere fact of the existence of such a relationship as naturally creates influence over the mind will lead the courts to infer the probability of undue influence having been exerted. Confidence has been held to imply the opportunity for influence, and when established, dispenses with any more direct proof of influence. In such cases the *onus* is cast upon the person occupying such a relationship to establish the perfect fairness and equity of the transaction. He must shew that the other acted after full and sufficient deliberation and with all the information that it was material for him to have, in order to guide his conduct, and that he had either independent and disinterested advice, or as ample protection as such advice could have given him (a). *Rhodes* v. *Bates* (b) lays it down that the donor must have had competent and independent advice.

The relation between a medical man and his patient is one in which the probability of undue influence is inferred;

---

(a) *Clarke* v. *Hawke*, 9 Grant, 52; *Denison* v. *Denison*, 13 Gr. 596; *Hoghton* v. *Hoghton*, 15 Beav. 299; *Haguenin* v. *Baseley*, 14 Ves. 300; Story, I Eq. Jur. sec. 314. But see *Andeureid's* Appeal, 89 Pa. St. 114; *McEwan* v. *Milne*, 5 Ont. R. 100.

(b) Law Rep. 1 Ch. 252.

and so in dealings with their patients the acts of physicians are watched with great jealousy; not because the Court blames and discountenances the influence flowing from such relation, but because it holds that this influence should be exerted for the benefit of the person subject to it, and not for the advantage of the person possessing it (c). The discontinuance of the relationship is only material if the influence has ceased with the relation; and the relation does not necessarily cease because the patient has not medicine actually administered to him at the time (d).

Where a surgeon and apothecary obtained from a patient, eighty-five years old, an agreement to pay him £25,000, in consideration of past medical services, duly charged and paid for, and the promise of future medical and surgical assistance until death without charge, and kept the matter concealed until after the death of the patient, the Court, on the prayer of the patient's executor, ordered the medical man to give up the agreement to be cancelled. So, when an octogenarian patient conveyed by deed of gift a property worth £1,000 to his physician, who was also his intimate friend, and the son of his benefactor, the Court set aside the deed for fraud. (In this case the consideration named in this deed was not the true one.) And even where a patient gave to his surgeon an annuity of £100 for the surgeon's life, in consideration that he would live with him and give him the benefit of his professional assistance during his (the donor's) life, it being shown that the surgeon had been told by an eminent physician, just before the deeds were drawn, that the patient could not recover or live long, and that the surgeon himself, about the same time, had said the patient could not live more than a month or so; the Court held the instruments could not be

(c) *Hoghton* v. *Hoghton*, sup.; *Dent* v. *Bennett*, 4 Myl. & C. 276; *Cadwallader* v. *West*, 48 Mo. 483.
(d) *Clarke* v. *Hawke*, sup.; *Dent* v. *Bennett*, sup.

maintained (e). A patient, aged, feeble, deaf and of very weak mind, bestowed all his estate on the attending physician, who lived with him, and had controlling influence over him, for an extremely trifling compensation. The transaction was set aside, the Court saying : " Owing to the relation which the parties sustained towards each other, the deed was presumptively the result of undue influence, and therefore *prima facie* void for that reason. It has been repeatedly declared by learned chancellors that the mere relation of patient and medical adviser was sufficient to avoid the contracts of the former made with the latter during the continuance of such relation " (f).

A security given by an old man for £262 10s. to a dentist, in consideration of his old teeth being kept in order and new ones being supplied during the remainder of his life, had to be given up (g). And if a man pays an exorbitant bill to a doctor, the Court will grant him relief; and it will be no answer to his asking his money back to say that he intended to be liberal, unless such intentions can be clearly shown (h). Even a sale to a patient by the medical man under whose care he is will be set aside if at an exorbitant price, and the purchaser has had no independent advice (i).

But where the evidence showed that the patient's own attorney prepared the papers, that he had independent advice, and understood what he was doing, and exercised his free will, and that the medical man had long attended him, the Court refused to set aside the deed, although the patient was eighty years of age (j). And although a

(e) *Dent* v. *Bennett,* sup.; *Gibson* v. *Russell,* 2 Y. & Coll. C. C. 104; *Popham* v. *Brooke,* 5 Russ. 104.
(f) *Cadwallader* v. *West,* 48 Mo. 483.
(g) *Allan* v. *Davis,* 4 De G. & Sim. 133.
(h) *Billage* v. *Southbee,* 9 Hare, 534, 540.
(i) *Peacock* v. *Kesnot,* 8 L. T. 292; *Wright* v. *Proud,* 13 Ves. 136.
(j) *Pratt* v. *Barker,* 1 Sim. 1.

gift made to a physician may be voidable, because of his standing in a confidential relation to the donor, a patient, yet, if after the confidential relation has ceased to exist, the donor intentionally elects to abide by the gift, and does, in fact, abide by it, it cannot be impeached after his death, even if it is not proved that the patient was aware that the gift was voidable at his election (*k*).

There is, of course, nothing in the relation of medical attendant and patient which can prevent the one from entering into a contract with the other, where the transaction proceeds openly and fairly, and the relation of physician and patient has, in reality, no bearing upon it (*l*). In the case of a sale by a patient to a physician, where there was no proof of inadequacy of price, the transaction was sustained (*m*).

A strong case must be made to set aside a will on the ground of undue influence. Influence is not sufficient: there must be such a degree of influence as deprives the testator of the proper mastery over his faculties (*n*). To invalidate a will, on the ground of undue influence, it must be shown that it was practised with respect to the will itself, or so contemporaneously with the will, or connected with it, as by almost necessary presumption to affect it; and flattery and obsequiousness, however degrading, will not constitute such an undue influence as will affect the acts of a capable testatrix (*o*). Many wills made in favour of medical men by their patients have been sustained, although disputed, and that even in cases where the patients have been aged, infirm women, with impaired minds (*p*).

(*k*) *Mitchell* v. *Homfray*, 8 Q. B. D. 587.
(*l*) *Aheare* v *Hogan*, Dru. 322.
(*m*) *Doggett* v. *Lane*, 12 Mo. 215.
(*n*) *Middleton* v. *Sherbourne*, 4 Y. & Coll. 358.
(*o*) *Jones* v. *Godrich*, 5 Moo. P. C. 16.
(*p*) *Farlar* v. *Lane*, 29 L. T. 2; *Jones* v. *Godrich*, 5 Moo. P. C. 16; *Reece* v. *Pressey*, 2 Jur. N. S. 380.

A physician, however, may fail to obtain the benefits which a grateful patient has wished him to have under a will, if—as was done in one case—after a long attendance on a patient, he thinks fit, when she is almost on her deathbed, to prepare and procure the execution of a will by which he becomes the principal object of her bounty, to the exclusion of her near relatives; and to do this without the intervention of any solicitor or other person competent to give her advice, and to guard her against undue influence; for in such a case the interests of the public require that his conduct should be regarded by Courts of Justice with the utmost jealousy (*q*). In another case, it was said that although there is no rule of law which forbids a man to bequeath his property to his medical attendant, yet it is not a favourable circumstance for one in such a confidential position, with respect to a patient labouring under a severe disease, to take a large benefit under such patient's will, more particularly, if it be executed in secrecy and the whole transaction assumes the character of a clandestine proceeding, and in such a case the *onus* will lie very heavily upon the party benefited to maintain the validity of the will (*r*).

Clairvoyant physicians may also get into trouble. An action was brought against one to set aside a marriage and a conveyance of property worth $25,000. The patient was old, feeble, deaf, childish and a firm spiritualist. The clairvoyant was a woman who pretended to be very modest and bashful and able to cure the deafness. After a course of treatment, mainly by manipulation, she told the old man that the spirits said that they must be married within two weeks, or something dreadful " would step in between them."

(*q*) *Greville* v. *Lylee*, 7 Moo. P. C. 320; *Durnell* v. *Corfield*, 3 L. T. 323; 1 Robarts, 51; *Major* v. *Knight*, 4 N. C. 661.

(*r*) *Ashwell* v. *Lomi*, L. R. 2 P. & D., 477. See also *Crispell* v. *Dubois*, 4 Barb. 393.

By misrepresentations concerning her character and her friends she won the old man and his property. After the honeymoon the patient came to his senses, and prayed to get back his liberty and possessions, because of the fraud used. The Court granted his prayer (s).

To promise a cure is unprofessional, and to obtain money on the faith of such a promise is sometimes dangerous. Brown falsely represented himself to A., an ignorant negro, to be a practising physician, and that he had restored sight to the blind. He persuaded A. that his (A.'s) house was infected with poison, and that it was in the bed occupied by his granddaughter, that she was poisoned, and that he could remove the poison if he was paid for so doing. A. gave him $22 to remove it. The Court held that Brown had been guilty of obtaining money under false pretences (t).

A physician should take all possible care to prevent the spread of smallpox or any other contagious disease, and use all such precautionary measures as may appear desirable. So, where the paper upon the walls of a room in which there had been smallpox patients had become so soiled and smeared with the smallpox virus as to make its removal necessary, a physician or other attendant may order the paper to be torn down; and the landlord cannot successfully maintain an action against the physician for doing this (u).

Apparently a surgeon may retain the limbs he cuts off a patient, upon the ground that parts of the body when severed become dead, and at common law there is no property in a dead human body. The point was once contested in Washington (v).

(s) *Hides* v. *Hides*, 65 How. Pr. Rep. 17; *Middleton* v. *Sherburne*, 4 Y. & Coll. 358.
(t) *Brown* v. *State*, 9 Baxter, 45.
(u) *Seavey* v. *Preble*, 64 Me. 120.
(v) 3 Co. Inst. 203; 20 A. L. J. 320.

A surgeon who attends a duel, although to save by his skill if possible the lives therein imperilled, will be held guilty of aiding and abetting the principal offender in the event of death ensuing (*w*).

If a medical practitioner wilfully injures a patient he is liable to be indicted for an assault, and if death ensue from the injuries so inflicted he may be indicted for murder. And this is so even though the patient might have submitted at the time from the supposition that the treatment was for his good. Having or attempting to have carnal connection with a female patient under pretence of treating her medically is an assault (*x*). Making a female patient strip naked, under pretence that the defendant, a medical practitioner, cannot otherwise judge of her illness, if he himself takes off her clothes, contrary to her wishes, is an assault. In this case the jury found that the defendant had stripped the girl wantonly, and not from any belief that it was necessary (*y*).

Where a physician takes an unprofessional unmarried man with him to attend a case of confinement, and no real necessity exists for the latter's assistance or presence, both are liable for damages; and it makes no difference that the patient, or her husband, supposed at the time that the intruder was a medical man, and therefore submitted without objection to his presence; or that the intruder accompanied the physician reluctantly on a dark and stormy night to carry a lantern or umbrella, and some instruments, and that there was only one room in the house. The Court remarked: "Dr. De May therefore took an unprofessional young unmarried man with him, introduced and permitted him to remain in the house of the plaintiff, when it was apparent that he could bear at least,

(*w*) *Reg.* v. *Cuddy*, 1 C. & K. 210; *Reg.* v. *Coney*, L. R. 8 Q. B. D. p. 569.
(*x*) *R.* v. *Case*, 19 L. J. M. C. 174; *R.* v. *Stanton*, 1 Car. & Kir. 415.
(*y*) *Rex* v. *Rosinski*, 1 Moo. C. C. 19.

if not see, all that was said and done, and, as the jury must have found under the instructions given, without either the plaintiff or her husband having any knowledge or reason to believe the true character of the third party. It would be shocking to our sense of right, justice and propriety even to doubt that for such an act the law would afford an ample remedy. To the plaintiff the occasion was a most sacred one, and no one had a right to intrude unless invited, or because of some real and pressing necessity which it is not pretended existed in this case. The plaintiff had a legal right to the privacy of her apartment at such a time, and the law secures to her this right by requiring others to observe it and to abstain from its violation. The fact that at the time she consented to the presence of Scattergood, supposing him to be a physician, does not preclude her from maintaining an action, and recovering substantial damages upon afterward ascertaining his true character. In obtaining admission at such a time and under such circumstances, without fully disclosing his true character, both parties were guilty of deceit, and the wrong thus done entitles the injured party to recover the damages afterward sustained, from shame and mortification, upon discovering the true character of the defendants." The action was brought by the wife (z).

If physicians, who have certified to the insanity of a person, have not made the enquiry and examination which the statute requires, or if their evidence and certificate in any respect of form or substance are not sufficient to justify a commitment to an asylum, the authorities should not commit, and if they do it is their fault and not that of the physicians, provided the latter have stated facts and opinions truly and have acted with due professional care and skill (a).

(z) *De May* v. *Roberts*, 46 Mich. 160; 41 Am. Rep. 154.
(a) *Pennell* v. *Cummings*, 75 Me.

If a medical man takes upon himself the responsibility of imprisoning a person on the ground of insanity, upon mere statements made to him by others, he will be liable to an action, and also for an assault, unless he can indeed show that the party imprisoned was insane at the time (*b*). He is not liable for an assault if he has signed a certificate under the Lunacy Acts and has done nothing more towards causing the confinement of the alleged lunatic (*c*). A medical man or other person may justify an assault where it is committed for the purpose of putting a restraint upon a dangerous lunatic in such a state that it is likely he may do mischief to some one (*d*).

In Ontario, except under order of the Lieutenant-Governor, no one can be admitted into a lunatic asylum without the certificate of three medical men, each attested by the signatures of two subscribing witnesses. Their certificates must state a personal and separate examination, and that after due enquiry the patient was found insane; and the physicians must also specify the facts upon which they formed their opinion of the insanity. In England, except in the case of paupers, two certificates are required (*e*).

The practice of abortion is forbidden by the oath of Hippocrates. The act is recognized as a crime in almost every code of medical ethics: its known commission has always been followed by ignominious expulsion from medical fellowship and fraternity. At Common Law a child *en ventre sa mere* is not considered a person the killing of whom is murder; but if one, intending to procure abortion, causes a child to be born so soon that it cannot live, and

---

(*b*) *Fletcher* v. *Fletcher*, 1 E. & E. 420; *Anderson* v. *Burrows*, 4 C. & P. 210.

(*c*) *Hall* v. *Semple*, 3 F. & F. 337.

(*d*) *Scott* v. *Wakem*, 3 F. & F. 333.

(*e*) R. S. O. cap. 220, secs. 8, 9; 16 & 17 Vict. cap. 96, secs. 4 & 5; (Imp. Stat.).

it dies in consequence, it is murder (*f*). And it is murder if one, attempting to procure abortion, either by means of drugs or instruments, cause the death of the woman (*g*).

In most civilized countries it is now either a felony, or grave misdemeanor, to attempt to procure the miscarriage of a woman by any means; or to supply or procure any thing knowing that it is intended to be unlawfully used or employed to procure a miscarriage (*h*). In some States the crime of abortion may be committed at any stage of pregnancy (*i*). The thing prescribed must be noxious in its nature, but it is not necessary to prove that it will produce miscarriage (*j*).

The burden of shewing that the use of instruments to produce abortion was necessary to save the life of the woman is on the accused (*k*).

It is an indictable offence for a physician, or any one else, unlawfully and injuriously to carry along or to expose in a public highway, on which persons are passing, and near to the habitations of others, any person infected with the small-pox, or any contagious disorder; and it is for the accused to shew that the object of the carrying or exposure was lawful (*l*).

In England, since 1840, it has been an indictable offence to innoculate for the small-pox (*m*). So, too, it has been in Canada for a number of years (*n*).

(*f*) *Reg.* v. *West*, 2 C. & K. 784.

(*g*) *R.* v. *West*, 2 C. & K. 784; *Mitchell* v. *Connor*, 78 Ky. 204; Russell on Crimes, vol. i. pp. 670, 740; *State* v. *Dickinson*, 41 Wis. 299.

(*h*) Imp. Stat. 24 & 25 Vict. cap. 100, secs. 58, 59; Can. Stat. 32 & 33 Vict. cap. 20, secs. 59, 60.

(*i*) *State* v. *Slagle*, 83 N. C. 630; *State* v. *Fitzgerald*, 49 Ia. 260.

(*j*) *State* v. *Gedicke*, 43 N. J. L. 86; *Reg.* v. *Fraser*, 9 Cox C. C. 228; *Reg.* v. *Hannah*, 13 Cox, C. C. 54.

(*k*) *Bradford* v. *People*, 20 Hun. (N. Y.) 309.

(*l*) *Rex.* v. *Burnett*, 4 M. & S. 272; *Rex.* v. *Sutton*, 4 Burr. 2116; *Rex.* v. *Vantandillo*, 4 M. & S. 73.

(*m*) 3 & 4 Vict. cap. 29, sec. 8; 30 & 31 Vict. cap. 84, sec. 32.

(*n*) 16 Vict. cap. 170, sec. 1.

It has been held in the State of Alabama, that where a special prohibitory Act does not except the practising physician from its operation, he is liable if he administers intoxicating bitters to his patient, but not for using liquors necessary in compounding medicine manufactured and sold by him. The application of any other rule, it was said by the Court, would be fraught with difficulty, if not impracticability. So, too, in Kansas (*o*).

Any registered practitioner who has been convicted of felony shall forfeit his right to registration, and the Medical Council may cause his name to be erased from the register; and if any one who has been convicted of felony presents himself for registration the registrar may refuse registration. But one's name cannot legally be removed from the register without notice and an opportunity of being heard (*p*).

A person who has met with personal injuries must exercise the same degree of care in the employment of a physician and surgeon, and in procuring and submitting to proper medical treatment, as a prudent and reasonable man would in any other matter; for those persons liable for the original injury will not be responsible for the further damage arising from the improper selection of a physician (*q*).

If a family doctor, or the surgeon of a company or society, on leaving home, recommends in case of need, some other physician, who is not, however, in any sense in his employment, it does not make him in any way liable for injuries arising from the latter's want of skill (*r*).

(*o*) *Carson* v. *State*, Ala. Sup. Ct. Dec. 1881; 25 A. L. J. 366; *State* v. *Kansas*, 29 Kans. 384; and see post Druggists.

(*p*) R. S. Ont. cap. 142, sec. 34; *Reg.* v. *Coll. of P. & S.*, 44 Ont. Q. B. 146.

(*q*) *Boynton* v. *Somersworth*, 58 N. H. 321.

(*r*) *Hitchcock* v. *Burgett*, 38 Mich. 501.

## CHAPTER XII.

### DISSECTION AND RESURRECTION.

A knowledge of the causes and nature of sundry diseases which affect the human body, and of the best methods of treating and curing such diseases, and of healing and repairing divers wounds and injuries to which the human frame is liable, cannot be acquired without the aid of anatomical examination. So saith the preamble to the British Anatomy Act of 1832. The chief hindrances to the pursuit of the study of anatomy have arisen from ignorance and superstition. A prejudice has prevailed in all nations against the violation of the human body after death. Even now, only philosophers like Jeremy Bentham are willing to have their bodies dissected by their friends. Simple association of thoughts causes the remains of a dead kinsman or friend to be treated with respect and tenderness; in the same way, the horror of death attaching to anything connected with the dead, and the religious idea that the soul outlives the body, and continues in a ghostly way to retain a connection with its old habitation of clay, have led to the respectful disposal of the corpse among most nations.

The Ptolemy princes Philadelphus and Euergetes, who enabled their physicians to dissect the human body, and prevented the prejudices of ignorance and superstition from compromising the welfare of the human race, were far in advance of their times. Long after their day, the Koran denounced as unclean the person who touched a corpse, and the rules of Islamism still forbid dissection; the old Moslem doctors only found opportunities of studying the bones of the human body in the cemeteries. Not until the days of Henry VIII. did the law make any provision for the cultivation and practice of the art of dissection. In 1540, more perhaps to strike terror into malefactors, than from any enlightened notion of forwarding knowledge, the Legislature gave permission to the masters of the Mystery of Barbers and Surgeons of London to take annually four persons, put to death for felony, for anatomies, and to make incision of the same dead bodies, or otherwise to order the same, after their discretions, at their pleasure, for their further insight and better knowledge, instruction, insight, learning, and experience, in the science or faculty of surgery (a).

Elizabeth, in 1565, made a similar grant to the College of Physicians, that they, observing all decent respect for human flesh, "might dissect the four felons." By 25 Geo. II. cap. 37 (1752), the bodies of all murderers executed in London and Westminster were to be given to the surgeons to be dissected and anatomised. But the legal supply of human bodies for anatomical examination still continued insufficient fully to provide the means of knowledge; and in order to furnish the necessary subjects, divers great and grievous crimes and murders were committed, the money paid, being the incentive. So, in 1832, the Anatomy Act (b) was passed. This Act proves clearly that Parliament regarded anatomy as a legal practice, and it provides for the licensing of those practising anatomy, allows any executor or other person, having lawful possession of any dead person (and not being an undertaker, etc.), to hand over the body for dissection (respect, however, being had to

(a) 32 Hy. VIII., cap. 42.
(b) 2 & 3 Wm. IV., cap. 75.

the wishes of the deceased or his known relatives). Inspectorships of schools of anatomy were likewise established.

In Canada, the bodies of convicts who die in a penitentiary, if unclaimed by the relatives, may be delivered to the professors of anatomy in any medical college, or to an inspector of anatomy (c).

The first defender of the faith, Henry VIII., the illustrious Elizabeth of most famous memory, and the enlightened James, had several statutes passed in which the disinterring of the dead is mentioned, but they were chiefly enactments against witchcraft, conjuration, the use of dead men's bones, and all sorts of sorceries. The parliament of James solemnly enacted, "that if any person should consult, covenant with, entertain, employ, feed or reward any evil and wicked spirit, to or for any intent or purpose, or take up any dead man, woman, or child out of his, her, or their grave, or any other place where the dead body rested, or the skin, bone, or any other part of any dead person, to be employed, or used, in any manner of witchcraft, sorcery, charm, or enchantment * * every such offender, his aiders, abettors, and counsellors, should suffer death as felons, and should lose the privilege and benefit of clergy and sanctuary" (d). This philosophical enactment graced the statute book until the ninth year of George II. While these statutes against sorcery were in force, and the Judges still imbued with the superstitious spirit of the age, the presumption was very strong that bodies disinterred were removed for purposes of enchantment or witchcraft, and resurrection-men and students of anatomy, as their aiders and abettors, were in imminent jeopardy of suffering as felons; but as the belief in sorcery grew weaker the prospect of these men grew brighter, and they were relieved from the great danger that they ran.

(c) 32 & 33 Vict., cap. 29, sec. 100.
(d) 1 Jac. I., cap. 12.

Under the laws of Constantine, a woman could without blame repudiate her husband, if he was guilty of violating the tombs of the dead; and we are told that the Ostrogoths allowed divorce for this same reason. And among the Franks, one who took the clothing from a buried corpse was banished from society, and none could relieve his wants until the relations of the deceased consented (*e*). As long ago as the tenth year of James I., at the assizes in Leicester, a man was tried for stealing winding sheets. Sir Edward Coke tells the matter thus: "One William Hain had in the night digged up the graves of divers several men and of one woman, and took the winding sheets from the bodies and buried the bodies again; and I advising hereupon, for the rareness of the case, consulted with the Judges at Sergeants' Inn on Fleet street, when we all resolved, that the property of the sheets was in the executors, administrators, or other owner of them, for the dead body is not capable of any property, and the property of the sheets must be in somebody, and according to this resolution he was indicted of felony in the next assizes; but the jury found it but petit larceny, for which he was whipped, as he well deserved." These learned people thought that if a winding sheet had been gratuitously furnished by a friend the property remained in the donor. For, quoth they, the winding sheet must be the property of somebody; a dead body, being but a lump of earth, hath no capacity; also, it is no gift to the person, but bestowed on the body for the reverence toward it, to express the hope of the resurrection; also, a man cannot relinquish the property he hath to his goods unless they be vested in another (*f*). Subsequently, lawyers have generally concurred in these opinions; the coffin, too, is the property of the personal representative of the deceased (*g*).

(*e*) 1 Russ. on Crimes, 465.
(*f*) 3 Inst. 110; 12 Co. 113 a.
(*g*) 2 East P. C. 652.

A still more interesting question arises as to who owns the corpse. It has been generally held that there is no property in it. Blackstone remarks, that, although the heir has a property in the monuments or escutcheons of his ancestor, he has none in his body or ashes. According to the law of England, after the death of a man, his executors have a right to the possession and custody of his body (although they have no property in it) until it is properly buried. A man cannot dispose of his body by will or any other instrument (*h*). A contract for the sale of a corpse, even to doctors, will not be enforced; it cannot be made an article of merchandise (*i*). The relatives have the right of interring the body, and when this right is once exercised they have no further interest in it than to protect it from injury (*j*). In Indiana, the Courts have diverged somewhat from the beaten track, and held that the surviving relatives are entitled to the corpse in the order of inheritance as property, and that they have a right to dispose of it as such, subject to whatever burial regulations are reasonable and proper for the public health and advantage (*k*).

The English Anatomy Act, as has been seen, gives the executor or other person having the lawful possession of the body of any deceased person power to permit it to be anatomically examined. In England, the earlier writers on criminal law say nothing of the taking of a body from the grave, except that it is not theft. East, however, calls it a great misdemeanor; and there have been several convictions for this as an offence at Common Law. Doubtless the belief that it was an offence at Common Law was nearly connected

---

(*h*) *Williams* v. *Williams*, L. R., 20 Ch. D. 659; *Reg.* v. *Sharpe*, Dea. and Bell, C. C. 160.

(*i*) Am. Law T., July, 1871.

(*j*) *Guthrie* v. *Weaver*, 1 Mo. App. 136; 4 Brady, 502; *Wynkoop* v. *Wynkoop*, 6 Wright, 293.

(*k*) *Bogert* v. *Indianapolis*, 13 Ind. 138.

with the idea of the bodies being used for the dark purposes of the necromancer, and it would appear that no distinct authority upon the abstract point has been found in ancient legal records (*l*). It is still an indictable offence, punishable with fine and imprisonment, or both (*m*). And this even though the body has been taken in the interest of science, and for the purpose of dissection; or even if the motives of the offender were pious and laudable. In *Lynn's* case—(Lynn was indicted for entering a burying ground, taking a coffin up, and carrying away a corpse for the purposes of dissection)—it was urged that the offence was cognizable only by the ecclesiastical courts; but the Judges of the King's Bench said that common decency required that a stop should be put to the practice; that it was an offence cognizable in a criminal court as being highly indecent, and *contra bonos mores*, at the bare idea alone of which nature revolted; that the purpose of taking up the body for dissection did not make it less an indictable offence. They refused to stay proceedings, but inasmuch as Lynn might have committed the deed merely through ignorance, they only fined him five marks. Since then others have been more severely dealt with. And in a very recent case, Stephen, J., said, "The law to be collected from these authorities seems to me to be this:—The practice of anatomy is lawful, though it may involve an unusual means of disposing of dead bodies, and though it certainly shocks the feelings of many persons; but to open a grave and disinter a dead body without authority is a misdemeanor, even if it is done for a laudable purpose."

It is, also, an indictable offence in many of the States to disinter a corpse, unless the deceased in his life-time had

(*l*) Willcock, cap. 10.

(*m*) 2 East P. Cr. 652; *R.* v. *Gilles,* Russ. & Ry. 366, n; *R.* v. *Lynn,* 2 T. R. 733; *Reg.* v. *Sharpe,* 1 D. & B. 160; *Reg.* v. *Price,* L. R. 12 Q. B. D. 247.

directed such a thing, or his relatives consent to it; and that the resurrecting is for the purpose of dissecting does not improve matters (*n*). In New York, removing dead bodies "for the purpose of selling the same," or "from mere wantonness," is punishable by both fine and imprisonment (*o*). And in New Hampshire and Vermont such offences bring upon those convicted, fines, whipping, and imprisonment, as the Court may see fit.

In Massachusetts, unclaimed dead bodies, and those of persons killed in duels, or capitally executed, are assigned to the medical schools of the State. The New York Act of 1789 must be considered as the first American Anatomy Law. The first section prohibits the removal of dead bodies for dissection, and the second section permits the Courts, in passing capital sentence, to award the body to the surgeons for dissection. Enactments similar to that of the New York Act, sec. 1, have been passed by the following States: Alabama, Arkansas, California, Connecticut, Georgia, Illinois, Indiana, Iowa, Kansas, Kentucky, Maine, Massachusetts, Michigan, Minnesota, Mississippi, Missouri, Nebraska, New Hampshire, Ohio, Oregon, Pennsylvania, Rhode Island, Tennessee, Texas, Vermont, Virginia, West Virginia, and Wisconsin. The second section of the New York Act has developed into the Acts of twenty-four States, which have thus legalized dissection, and most of them have made specific provision for the dissection of the bodies of certain deceased criminals, chiefly murderers. ; these States are Alabama, Arkansas, California, Colorado, Connecticut, Georgia, Illinois, Indiana, Iowa, Kansas, Maine, Massachusetts, Michigan, Minnesota, Missouri, Nebraska, New Hampshire, New Jersey, New York, Ohio, Pennyslvania, Tennessee, Vermont, and Wisconsin. Some of these States

---

(*n*) *Tate v. State*, 6 Black. (Ind.) 111; *Com. v. Loring*, 8 Pick. (Mass.) 370; *Com. v. Marshall*, 11 Pick. 350; *Com. v. Cooley*, 10 Pick. 37.

(*o*) 2 R. S. 688, sec. 13.

have made no other provision for anatomical study beyond that mentioned (*p*). We have already referred to the Canadian Act on this subject. In addition, the Ontario Act provides that the bodies of persons found dead, publicly exposed, or who at time of death had been supported in and by some institution receiving government aid (except lunatics in provincial asylums), shall, unless the person so dying otherwise direct, or the *bona fide* friends or relations claim it, be given to public medical schools in the locality, or to public teachers of anatomy or surgery, or private medical practitioners, having three or more pupils, for whose instruction such bodies are actually required. Such medical practitioners must give security for the decent interment of the bodies after they have served their purposes; and then a written authority to open a dissecting room is given by the Inspector of Anatomy of the city, town, or place. The Inspector's duty is to keep a register of bodies given up for dissection; a register of the qualified practitioners desiring bodies; to make an impartial distribution of the bodies in rotation; to visit the dissection rooms, and to report to the police magistrate or chief municipal officer, any improper conduct on the part of students or teachers (*q*).

A person may be found guilty of the offence of disinterring a corpse, even though he was not actually present at the body-lifting, if with the intention of giving aid and assistance he was near enough to afford it, if required (*r*).

Besides the danger he runs of being brought before a criminal tribunal, the body-lifter incurs the risk of civil proceedings being taken against him. It is true, as Blackstone says, the heir has no property in the body or ashes of

(*p*) 23 Albany L. J. 421.
(*q*) R. S. O. cap. 143.
(*r*) *Tate* v. *State*, 6 Black. 111.

his ancestors; nor can he bring any civil action against such as indecently, at least, if not impiously, violate and disturb their remains when dead and buried; but that learned commentator goes on to remark: "The person, indeed, who has the freehold of the soil, may bring an action of trespass against such as dig and disturb it" (s). This has been clearly established in a case in Massachusetts, where a father sued for the removal of the remains of his child, and recovered a verdict for $837 in an action of trespass *quare clausum fregit*. Mr. Justice Forster, in giving judgment, remarks that a dead body is not the subject of property, and after burial it becomes part of the ground to which it has been committed, earth to earth, dust to dust, ashes to ashes. The only action that can be brought is trespass *quare clausum*. Any one, said the Judge, in actual possession of the land may maintain this against a wrong-doer. The gist of the action is the breaking and entering, but the circumstances which accompany and give character to the trespass may always be shown either in aggravation or mitigation. Acts of gross carelessness as well as those of wilful mischief often inflict a serious wound to the feelings, when the injury done to property is comparatively trifling, and we know of no rule of law which requires the mental suffering of the party complaining, caused by the misconduct of the wrong-doer, to be disregarded (t).

Willcock, in his "Laws relating to the Medical Profession," in his tenth chapter, when considering the lawfulness or unlawfulness of taking bodies for the purpose of dissection, says: "The whole question must depend upon the proper answer to these inquiries. Is it a violation of property?

---

(s) 2 Com. 429.

(t) *Meagher v. Driscoll*, 99 Mass. 281; *Barnstable v. Thatcher*, 3 Metc. 243; *Bracegirdle v. Orford*, 2 M. & S. 77; *Brewer v. Dero*, 11 M. & W. 625.

Is it a personal injury to any individual? Or is it an injury to the public? Every lawyer who has mentioned the subject has admitted that there is no violation of property in respect of the corpse itself, which is necessary to constitute the removal an offence; and Blackstone has distinctly stated that the only property violated is the grass and soil of the land wherein the body was interred, in respect of which the person may bring his action of trespass, and the law has not provided any punishment as for an offence. It is equally clear that it is not an injury to any person; for the shrewd lawyers of Coke's time determined that the body was no person but a lump of clay; and the only injury which can give a right of action to—that is which amounts to a violation of any legal right of—a relative or master, is such as may be said to recoil upon him, by causing him expense, labor, or loss of valuable service. The unpleasantness which may arise from an attack upon prejudices, however intimately blended with good feeling and delicacy of sentiment, is ranked by the court with that class of wrongs which are technically designated *damna absque injuria*."

"In *Lynn's* case, the judges assumed to answer the third question, that is to assert that it is an injury to the public. Society is not injured by the disinterment of the dead for the purposes of science, for it could hardly exist without such a sacrifice of fastidiousness; society is not insulted by the secret abstraction of the corpse from the vermin which crowd to pollute it, and they who so curiously seek the remains of those they hold dear, behind the veil of science, would do well to pry for one moment into the secrets of the sepulchre. They alone are the violators of every sentiment of delicacy and benevolence who insult the disconsolate relatives with the tale of the robbery and the pursuit, and with the foul spectacle of dismemberment they may have at length discovered."

It would appear that in a proper case the Court, in the interests of justice, will compel the exhuming and examination of a dead body which is under the control of a plaintiff, if there is strong reason to believe that without such examination a fraud is likely to be accomplished, and the defendant has exhausted every other method known to the law of exposing it. However, such an order should be made only upon a strong showing to that effect. "It would be a proceeding repugnant to the best feelings of our nature, and likely to be in many cases so abhorrent to the sensibilities of the surviving relatives, that they would prefer an abandonment of the suit to a compliance with the order." Thus spake the court in a case where the order for exhuming was asked for and refused as not being justified under the circumstances. The action was on a policy of insurance, and the defence was, that the insured had falsely warranted that he had never received any serious personal injury, whereas his skull had been fractured in boyhood, and had been healed by trephining. To prove this, the company proposed to disinter his body, after the suit had been pending eighteen months, upon the sole testimony of his physician, that the deceased had said that he had been told of such an accident and operation. The counsel for the plaintiff called the proposal "revolting," and said that to break the signet of the grave, and take from its resting place the sacred property of relatives to gratify the corporation's mercenary curiosity, would be worse than Shylock's demand (*u*).

(*u*) *Granger's Ins. Co.* v. *Brown*, 57 Miss. 308.

## CHAPTER XIII.

### DENTISTS.

The need of dentists existed long before dentistry. The Preacher knew of the inconveniences which arise when the grinders are few. Marcellus, about B. C. 380, gave two receipts for toothache. One is, "Say, 'argidam, margidam, sturgidam;'" the other is, "Spit in a frog's mouth and request him to make off with the complaint." These are given in Glenn's "Laws affecting Medical Men."

In England, in the tenth and eleventh centuries, priests and monks were the dentists of the day. Afterwards, a decree of the Council of Tours having forbad clergymen undertaking or engaging in any bloody operation, all surgical practice fell into the hands of blacksmiths and barbers. The latter soon became the more important class, and in 1461 (as we have seen already), Edward IV. incorporated them as "The Freeman of the Mystery or Faculty of Surgery." By degrees other persons assumed to practise pure surgery, and these two bodies, in 1560, were united by Act of Parliament, and became "The Masters or Governors of the Mystery and Commonalty of the Barbers and Surgeons of London." By the third section of this Act (a), because of fear of the spread of contagious diseases, any one in the City of London using barbery or shaving, was forbidden to

---

(a) 32 Henry VIII. cap. 42.

occupy any surgery, letting of blood, or any other thing belonging to surgery, drawing of teeth only excepted. In those days one wishing to find a drawer of teeth had to resort to one of those shops where was exhibited the bandaged pole as a sign or symbol that "all the King's liege people there passing by might know at all times whither to resort in time of necessity."

Something more than a sign is now required of dental surgeons. The Royal College of Surgeons in England has now the power to appoint examiners for testing the fitness of persons to practise as dentists, and to grant certificates of such fitness. To become a Licentiate of Dental Surgery in England, it is necessary to be engaged for four years in the acquirement of professional knowledge; to attend at a recognized school one course of lectures, at least, in anatomy, physiology, surgery, medicine, chemistry, and materia medica, and a second course on the anatomy of the head and neck; one course on metallurgy, and two on dental surgery and anatomy, dental physiology and mechanics; to have dissected for nine months; to have taken a course of chemical manipulation; to have attended a hospital for two or more sessions; and to have spent three years in acquiring practical familiarity in mechanical dentistry under a competent practitioner; and then to pass the examination required by the board.

In Ontario, "The Royal College of Dental Surgeons" has power to appoint a Board of Directors, who have authority to fix the curriculum of studies to be pursued by students, to determine the period during which they must be employed under a practitioner, to appoint the examiners, and arrange the examinations, for those who desire to obtain a license to practise dental surgery in the province. The Board may also confer the title of "Master of Dental Surgery" upon any licentiate who passes certain examinations and conforms with certain regulations. The College is composed of all those entitled to practise in the Province; and no one who is not a member of the College can practise dentistry for hire, gain or hope of reward, or pretend to hold, or take, or use any name, title, addition or description, implying that he holds a license to practise, or that he is a member of the College, or shall falsely represent, or use any title representing that he is a graduate of any dental college, under a penalty of $20 and costs for every offence, to be recovered in a summary way before a magistrate, or in a Division Court by suit. Persons contravening the Act cannot recover for work done or materials provided. Of course, the Act does not interfere with legally qualified medical practitioners (*b*).

Dentists are subject to the same rules, as to negligence, as are physicians or surgeons (*c*), and if by a culpable want of attention and care, or by the absence of a competent degree of skill and knowledge, a D.D.S. causes injury to a patient, he is liable to a civil action for damages, unless, indeed, such injury be the immediate result of intervening negligence on the part of the patient himself, or unless such patient has by his own carelessness directly conduced to the injury (*d*). The law is ever reasonable; so it only requires of a dentist a reasonable degree of care and skill in his professional operations, and will not hold him answerable for injuries arising from his want of the highest attainments in his profession. The rule is, that the least amount of skill with which a fair proportion of the practitioners of a given locality are endowed, is the criterion by which to judge of the professional man's ability or skill (*e*). As far as the liability is concerned, no distinction is made

(*b*) R. S. O. cap. 144.
(*c*) *Simonds* v. *Henry*, 39 Me. 153.
(*d*) Glenn's Laws, p. 251.
(*e*) McClelland's Civil Malpractice, p. 19.

between those who are regular practitioners and those who are not so; the latter are equally bound with the former to have and to employ competent skill and attention.

A patient must exercise ordinary care and prudence (*f*); so that, if one tells the dentist to pull out a tooth, but does not say which one is to go, and the wrong one is taken out, the sufferer has no legal ground of complaint, unless, indeed, it is quite apparent which is the offending member. A patient may have been a little careless and negligent; still, if the dentist has been so very neglectful of his duty that no ordinary care on the part of the patient would have prevented the mistake or injury complained of, the injured party will recover, *i.e.*, recover damages for the injury received (*g*).

The fact that one has taken chloroform will not affect his rights or remedies against the tooth-puller for any mistake or negligence. The maxim *vigilantibus, non somnientibus jura subveniunt*, has no reference to people put to sleep by anæsthetics. In New York, two dentists undertook to extract a tooth from a patient while the latter was under the influence of laughing gas. During the operation the forceps slipped, and part of the tooth went down the patient's throat, causing coughing and vomiting for four weeks, when—in a fit of coughing—the tooth came up, and relief followed. The patient sued for damages, and when the case came before it, the Court said, " The defendants (the dentists) knew that the plaintiff (the patient) while under the influence of the anæsthetic, had no control of his faculties, that they were powerless to act, and that he was unable to exert the slightest effort to protect himself from any of the probable or possible consequences of the operation which they had undertaken to perform. He was in their

(*f*) *Eakin* v. *Brown,* 1 E. D. Smith, 36.
(*g*) *Clarke* v. *Kerwin,* 4 E. D. Smith, 21 : *Parker* v. *Adams,* 12 Metc. 417.

charge and under their control to such an extent that they were required to exercise the highest professional skill and diligence to avoid every possible danger; for the law imposes duties upon men according to the circumstances in which they are called to act. In this case, skill and diligence must be considered as indissolubly associated. The professional man, no matter how skilful, who leaves an essential link wanting, or a danger unguarded in the continuous chain of treatment, is guilty of negligence, and if the omission results in injury to the patient, the practitioner is answerable. The quantum of evidence necessary to make out a *primâ facie* case of negligence is very slight in some cases, while in others a more strict proof is required. Often the injury itself affords sufficient *primâ facie* evidence of negligence. * * * There was evidence offered by the plaintiff showing, that while the defendant drew the tooth, the forceps slipped. This fact, combined with the unusual circumstance that the tooth went down instead of coming up, was sufficient to carry the case to the jury upon the question of negligence. The trial Judge held that while the affirmative was upon the plaintiff to prove negligence, the fact that the defendants, instead of taking the plaintiff's tooth out, let it go down his throat, was sufficient evidence to carry the question of negligence to the jury, to the enp that they might determine whether, in the light of all the circumstances, the defendants had exercised the skill and care which the exigencies of the case required. This ruling was correct" (h).

Boyle's case is an interesting one on the subject of the use of chloroform. He was a street-car driver; a vicious horse by a kick threw him from his platform, so that he hit his head against a tree-box. He was picked up insensible and carried into a surgery; this he was enabled to leave

(h) *Keily* v. *Cotton*. 26 Alb. L. J. 483.

in a couple of hours, and the following day went to work again. In course of time he had a toothache, and went to a Dr. Winslow's to have it extracted, intending to take chloroform. The chloroform was administered, but did not operate as soon as usual, exciting rather than tranquilizing B. Insensibility, however, having been finally obtained, the teeth were taken out, the doctor giving the anæsthetic from time to time during the operation, as symptoms of returning consciousness appeared. Boyle walked home shortly afterwards, feeling, however, dizzy, and being uncertain in his gait; these unpleasant symptoms continued even after reaching his house. The next day, thickness of speech and numbness of one arm and side came on, with partial paralysis. From this he was still suffering, when a jury was called upon to say whether his state was due to the neglect of the dentist or not. The Judge told the jury that, even if they doubted the safety of the agent employed (chloroform), there was still a consideration of the highest reason which they ought not to disregard. He remarked, "All science is the result of a voyage of exploration, and the science of medicine can hardly be said to have yet reached the shore. Men must be guided therefore by what is probably true, and are not responsible for their ignorance of the absolute truth which is not known. If a medical practitioner resorts to the acknowledged proper sources of information—if he sits at the feet of masters of high reputation and does as they have taught him—he has done his duty, and should not be made answerable for the evils that may result from errors in the instruction which he has received. * * * He who acts according to the best known authority is a skilful practitioner, although that authority should lead him in some respects wrong. * * * If the plaintiff was from previous circumstances predisposed to paralysis, it might well happen that the extraction of his teeth, without the chloroform, or the use of the chloroform without the extraction, would bring on a paralytic attack. Even if this was the case, still it would not be just to make the defendant answerable for consequences which he could not foresee, which were not the ordinary or probable result of what he did. He was only bound to look to what was natural and probable, to what might reasonably be anticipated. Unless such guard is thrown around the physician his judgment may be clouded, or his confidence shaken by the dread of responsibility, at those critical moments when it is all important that he should retain the free and undisturbed enjoyment of his faculties, in order to use them for the benefit of the patient " (*i*).

In the olden time, front teeth were considered very valuable. Our ancestors appear to have used them in fighting, and the hurting of a man so as to render him less able in fighting to defend himself or annoy his adversary, was considered a misdemeanor of the highest kind, and spoken of by my Lord Coke as the greatest offence under felony. To cut off an ear or strike off a nose was nothing to the knocking out of a fore-tooth, for a nose or an ear is useless in a fight—doubtless they are in the way (*j*). According to that system of punishment introduced into England by the Engles, which compensated every injury by a money payment, a front tooth was valued highly, and one who deprived another of such a member had to pay six shillings, while breaking a rib only cost half as much, and shattering a thigh only twelve shillings (*k*).

The fact that a dentist extracts teeth for love and not for money does not relieve him of his liability for failure to perform his work properly (*l*); and if one is foolish enough

(*i*) *Boyle* v. *Winslow*, 5 Phil. (Pa.) 136.
(*j*) Russell on Crimes, vol. I. p. 720.
(*k*) Taswell-Langmead, English Constit. History, p. 41.
(*l*) *Street* v. *Blackburn*, 1 H. Bl. 159; *Wilson* v. *Brett*, 11 M. & W. 113.

to allow an ignorant apprentice to practise on his teeth, he can still recover from the dentist for any injuries (*m*). It is a good answer to an action brought by a dentist to recover payment for his work and labor, that the defendant has been injured instead of benefited by the plaintiff's treatment, either because of his want of skill or his negligence. So, when Mr. Gilpin went to Mr. Wainwright to have a tooth extracted, and Wainwright gave him chloroform, and then pulled out the wrong tooth, and Gilpin declined to pay for the performance, alleging a want of consideration, the dentist sued for his account, but the Court gave judgment against him (*n*). If the dentist's bill has been increased owing to his own mistake or wrong doing—as where being employed to pull out one tooth and insert a false one, he pulled out two, and so had to put in two; he cannot recover for this additional amount of work. Lord Kenyon well put this when he said : " If a man is sent for to extract a thorn which might be pulled out with a pair of nippers, and through his misconduct it becomes necessary to amputate the limb, shall it be said, that he may come into a court of justice to recover fee for the cure of the wound which he himself has caused ?" (*o*). To put the question is to give the answer. In fact, in such a case as the one put, it would appear that not only could no recovery be had for the additional services rendered necessary by the dentist's own want of proper care, but the man whose grinders were thus made few would be entitled to a further deduction from the bill for the bodily suffering and damage he had sustained (*p*).

One cannot reasonably expect to have teeth as well fitted to the mouth by art as nature. Mrs. Henry got a set of artificial ones from Dr. Simonds; when put into her

---

(*m*) *Hancke* v. *Hooper*, 7 C. & P. 81.

(*n*) Glenn's Laws, p. 209.

(*o*) Peake's N. P. C. 83, 84.

(*p*) *Piper* v. *Menifee*, 12 B. Monr. 465.

mouth, she complained that they felt odd and pained her. The plate was somewhat filed, but she was still dissatisfied, and declined to pay the bill. It was then agreed that she should take them away and try them for a day or two; this was done, and again she returned them, declining to pay. The doctor then sued, and the evidence as to whether the teeth fitted was conflicting. One testified that they were a good piece of work; another, that they were a fair average piece of work; while a third said that they were nothing extra. The Judge instructed the jury that if Simonds had used all the knowledge and skill to which the art had at the time advanced, that would be all that could be required of him. The verdict was for the defendant. On an application for a new trial the court considered the instructions erroneous and granted a new trial, saying: "that surgeons are held responsible for injuries resulting from a want of ordinary care and skill. The highest degree of skill is not to be expected, nor can it reasonably be required, of all. The instruction given was * * * undoubtedly correct, and no more would be required of him. But, upon legal principles, could so much be required of him? We think not. If it could, then every professional man would be bound to possess the highest attainment, and to exercise the greatest skill in his profession. Such a requirement would be unreasonable" (*q*).

It is a dangerous thing for both parties for the dentist to try a new instrument or a new *modus operandi* for the first time—doing so the Court once said was a rash act, and he who acts rashly acts ignorantly. Using a new instrument is acting contrary to the known rule and usage of the profession (*r*). One cannot become an experimentalist except at his own peril.

(*q*) *Simonds* v. *Henry*, 39 Me. 155.
(*r*) *Slater* v. *Balter*, 2 Wils. 359, 362.

A dentist, at a lady's request, prepared a model of her mouth, and made two sets of artificial teeth for her. In response to a letter notifying her that they were ready, and asking when he could come and put them in, the dentist received the following note: "My dear Sir, I regret, after your kind effort to oblige me, my health will prevent my taking advantage of the early day. I fear I may not be able for some days. Yours, etc., Frances P." Very shortly the lady died. The dentist sued her executors for £21, but he failed to recover. The court held that a contract to make a set of teeth is a contract for the sale of goods, wares or merchandise within the meaning of the seventeenth section of the Statute of Frauds; and that as by the terms of the contract the teeth were to be fitted to the lady's mouth, and as this, through no default on her part, was never done, her executors were not liable to the dentist for work done and materials provided; nor was the letter a sufficient memorandum within the meaning of the Act referred to. Counsel for the plaintiff and the Court seemed to differ widely in their opinions of the artistic nature of tooth-making. The former, arguing that the deceased had in truth contracted for the skill of the dentist, and that the materials were merely auxiliary to the work and labour, said this case was not to be distinguished from that of an artist employed to paint a picture; the ivory used was of insignificant value as compared to the skill employed. Judge Crompton, however, said: "Here the subject matter of the contract was the supply of goods. The case bears a strong resemblance to that of a tailor supplying a coat, the measurement of the mouth and the fitting of the teeth being analogous to the measurement and fitting of the garment" (s).

A similar view of the standing of a dentist was taken by the Court in Michigan, when it held that he was a "mechanic." The Court observed, "A dentist, in one sense, is

(s) *Lee* v. *Griffin*, 1 E. B. & S. 272.

a professional man, but, in another sense, his calling is mainly mechanical, and the tools which he employs are used in mechanical operations. Indeed, dentistry was formerly purely mechanical, and instruction in it scarcely went beyond manual dexterity in the use of tools; and a knowledge of the human system generally, and of the diseases which might affect the teeth and render an operation important, was by no means considered necessary. Of late, however, as the physiology of the human system has become better understood, and the relations of the various parts and their mutual dependence become more clearly recognized, dentistry has made great progress as a science, and its practitioners claim, with much justice, to be classed among the learned professions. It is nevertheless true that the operations of the dentist are, for the most part, mechanical, and so far as tools are employed, they are purely so, and we could not exclude these tools from the exemption which the statute makes, without confining the construction of the statute within limits not justified by the words employed"(t). On the other hand, in Mississippi, the Court said, " A dentist cannot be properly denominated a ' mechanic.' It is true that the practice of his art requires the use of instruments for manual operations, and that much of it consists in manual operations; but it also involves a knowledge of the physiology of the teeth, which cannot be acquired but by a proper course of study, and this is taught by learned treatises upon the subject, and as a distinct though limited part of the medical art, in institutions established for the purpose. It requires both science and skill, and if such persons should be included in the denomination of 'mechanics,' because their pursuit required the use of mechanical instruments and skill in manual operation, the same reason would include general surgeons under the same denomination, because the prac-

(t) *Maxon* v. *Perrott*, 17 Mich. 332.

tice of their profession depends in a great degree upon similar instruments and operative skill; nor could such a pursuit properly be said to be a trade " (*u*).

False teeth have been considered necessaries for a wife. One Andrews had a conversation with Gilman, a dentist, as to the latter furnishing the former's wife with a plate of mineral teeth, and he agreed to pay for certain other dental services rendered to Mrs. A. The plate was furnished while Mr. and Mrs. A. were living together, and it was quite suitable to the former's circumstances and station in life; he saw it, knew whence it came, raised no objection to it, still he declined to pay for it. The Court, however, held him liable, not only because the wife being permitted to retain the plate, and the other circumstances, showed her authority to make the purchase, but also on the ground that the teeth were some of those necessaries wherewith a husband is bound to furnish his wife (*v*).

A dentist must not take any unfair advantage of his patient. Some thirty years ago, one Captain Simpson, a very old seaman and a pensioner in Greenwich Hospital, gave a bill of exchange, payable eight months after date, for £262 10s. to one Davis, a London dentist, purporting to be for value received. Davis said, the real bargain was that he should during the whole of the Captain's life attend to his teeth, and supply him with new ones from time to time. He also said that a new set of teeth would cost from £30 to £50. The bill was in the handwriting of D.; it was given in his house when no third person was by, and it was never heard of until after the captain's death, which took place before it was due. There was no writing as to the teeth. The executors of Simpson declined to pay, whereupon Davis handed the note over to a creditor of his own,

---

(*u*) *Whitcomb* v. *Reid*, 31 Miss. 567.
(*v*) *Gilman* v. *Andrews*, 28 Vt. 24.

who sued both parties. The executors filed a bill in chancery, impeaching the document for fraud, and asking that it might be delivered up to them. The Court thought that it was quite impossible for any reasonable being to draw any inference from the materials before it, but that it was a case of fraud—nay, a gross fraud, and the decree was made as asked (*w*). Sir Launcelot Shadwell thought that the case had points of resemblance to that of *Dent v. Bennett* (*x*), in which a medical man bargained for a very large sum of money to attend a person of advanced years until death; but in that case the doctor had to attend to the whole human body, not merely to a particular part of it.

One dentist must not imitate too closely the sign or card of a fellow practitioner. One Colton alleged that he had purchased from a Dr. G. Q. Colton the right to use the name "Colton Dental Association" in connection with the use of nitrous-oxide gas to alleviate pain in the extraction of teeth, and that he used the same in advertisements and prominently displayed it on signs; that the defendant, who had been in his employment, left him, opened dental rooms in the same street, issued cards announcing that he was "formerly operator at the Colton Dental Rooms," and extracted teeth without pain by the use of nitrous-oxide gas, and put a sign to the same purport over his door, but the words "formerly operator at the," upon cards and sign, were in small and almost illegible letters, while the words "Colton Dental Rooms" were very conspicuous; the signs were very similar in shape, size, &c., and were hung on the same side of the street, in the same manner, and might readily be mistaken the one for the other, especially by suffering patients impatient for relief. An injunction against the defendant's cards and signs was granted (*y*).

(*w*) *Allen* v. *Davis*, 4 DeG. & S. 133.
(*x*) 4 My. & C. 269.
(*y*) *Colton* v. *Thomas*, 2 Brews. 308.

And where Morgan and Schuyler, two dentists, dissolved partnership, S. bought M.'s interest in the fixtures and in the lease of the room, and continued business therein. M. removed his name from the sign, but S. replaced it, and put above, in letters so small as to be nearly imperceptible, his own name with the words "successor to." The agreement of dissolution did not prohibit M. from engaging in the business, so he opened an office therefor in another part of the city. He then applied to the Court to restrain his late partner from the use of his name as mentioned. He was successful in his action. But the Court thought that S. would have kept with his rights if he had merely described himself as "late of" the firm (z).

(z) *Morgan* v. *Schuyler*, 79 N. Y. 490; S. C. 35 Am. Rep. 543.

## CHAPTER XIV.

### DRUGGISTS.

A druggist, the Supreme Court of Louisiana says, means "one who sells drugs without compounding or preparing them: and so is a more limited term than apothecary (*a*)."

A commission merchant, dealing principally in alcohol, is not a druggist, within the meaning of the Massachusetts' Act, regulating the sale of alcohol by druggists (*b*); and although whiskey may be sold by druggists in comparatively small quantities as medicine, and doubtless a great many people so take it, still it was held that fifty barrels of whiskey remaining in a bonded warehouse at the time of his death would not pass under the will of a wholesale and retail druggist bequeathing his stock of medical drugs, etc. The Court considered fifty barrels of whiskey wholly disproportionate to the ordinary stock of medicine and drugs kept on hand by the testator—too much sack for the bread (*c*). One may be an apothecary or druggist although he does not actually compound his medicines (*d*).

In the early days in England, the grocers, or poticaries, who formed one of the trade guilds of London, united with their ordinary business the sale of such ointments, simples

---

(*a*) *State* v. *Holmes*, 28 La. Ann. 765.
(*b*) *Mills* v. *Perkins*, 120 Mass. 41.
(*c*) *Klock* v. *Burger*, 50 Md. 575.
(*d*) *Haniline* v. *Commonwealth*, 13 Bush. 350.

and medicinal compounds as were then in use. In the days of Henry VIII., the medical department of the grocers' trade being greatly increased, shops were established for the exclusive sale of drugs and medicinal and all kinds of chemcial preparations. We have a graphic description of one of these apothecaries about the days of "Good Queen Bess," in the words of the prince of English dramatists:

>    ——I do remember an apothecary,
> And hereabouts he dwells, which late I noticed
> In tatter'd weeds, with overwhelming brows,
> Culling of simples : meagre were his looks,
> Sharp misery had worn him to the bones,
> And in his needy shop a tortoise hung,
> An alligator stuff'd, and other skins
> Of ill-shaped fishes : and about his shelves
> A beggarly account of empty boxes,
> Green earthen pots, bladders and musty seeds,
> Remnants of pack thread and old cakes of roses
> Were thinly scattered to make up a show.
>              ROMEO AND JULIET, Act. V., sc. I.

Until 1868, any person whatever might open what is called a chemist's shop in England, and deal in drugs and poisons. In that year, however, the Pharmacy Act was passed, which prohibits any person engaging in the business of, or assuming the title of, Chemist and Druggist, or dispensing chemicals or drugs, unless he be registered under that Act. And to be registered one must pass an examination in Latin, English, arithmetic, prescriptions, practical dispensing, pharmacy, materia medica, botany and chemistry.

Under the Ontario Act (c) there is a College of Pharmacy, managed by a Pharmaceutical Council who grant certificates of competency to practise as pharmaceutical chemists, prescribe the subjects on which candidates are to be ex-

(c) R. S. O. cap. 145.

amined, and arrange for the registration of chemists. No one, save those registered or their employeés, is authorized to compound prescriptions of legally authorized medical practitioners. The Act, however, does not apply to medical practitioners. But, save as aforesaid, no one can retail, dispense, or compound poisons, or sell certain articles named, or assume or use the title of "Chemist and Druggist," or "Chemist," or "Druggist," or "Pharmacist or Apothecary," or "Dispensing Chemist or Druggist," unless he has complied with the Act.

The Code Napoleon recognizes two classes of vendors of drugs and medicines, apothecaries and druggists. The former, who are assumed to be pharmaceutically educated, are alone allowed to sell compounded medicine, the latter who are classed with grocers are only permitted to sell drugs of a simple character in bulk and at wholesale (*f*). In the United States, wherever statutes do not otherwise direct, apothecaries and druggists are put upon the common law footing of provision vendors, and may sell in any quantities articles in which they deal.

A druggist is held to a strict accountability in law for any mistake he may make in compounding medicine or selling his drugs. By the statute law of England it is declared to be the duty of every person using or exercising the art or mystery of an apothecary to prepare with exactness, and to dispense, such medicines as may be directed for the sick by any physician (*g*). And by the same Act, for the further protection, security, and benefit of George the Third's subjects it was declared, that if any one using the art or mystery of an apothecary, should deliberately or negligently, unfaithfully, fraudulently or unduly make, mix, prepare or sell any medicines, as directed by any prescription signed by any

---

(*f*) Code of Med. Pol. 332, 333.
(*g*) 55 Geo. III., cap. 194, sec, 5.

licensed physician, such apothecary shall, on conviction before a Justice of the Peace, unless good cause be shown to the contrary, forfeit for the first offence £5, for second, £10, and for third he shall forfeit his certificate. But apart from any statute, whenever a druggist or apothecary (using the words in their general sense) sells a medicine, he impliedly warrants the good quality of the drugs sold; and besides that, he warrants that it is the article that is required and that it is compounded in every prescription dispensed by him *secundum artem*. Like the provision dealer, the pharmaceutist is bound to know that the goods he sells are sound, *i.e.*, competent to perform the mission required of them, and being so presumed to know, he warrants their good qualities by the very act of selling them for such. The rule, "Let the buyer beware," does not apply.

In some way Fleet and Simple got cantharides mixed with some snake root and Peruvian bark. Unfortunately Hollenbeck, requiring some of this latter mixture, bought this that these druggists had, took it as a medicine, and in consequence suffered great pain, and had his health permanently impaired. He sued for damages, and recovered a verdict for $1,140. The defendants asked for a new trial, but the Court refused it saying, "Purchasers have to trust to a druggist. It is upon his skill and prudence they must rely. It is his duty to know the properties of his drugs, to be able to distinguish them from one another. It is his duty so to qualify himself, or to employ those who are so qualified, to attend to the business of compounding and vending medicines and drugs, as that one drug may not be sold for another; and so that, when a prescription is presented to be made up the proper medicine, and none other, be used in mixing and compounding it. The legal maxim should be reversed, instead of *caveat emptor* it should be *caveat vendor*, *i.e.*, let him be certain that he does not sell to a purchaser or send to a patient, one thing for another, as arsenic for calomel, cantharides for, or mixed with snake root and Peruvian bark, or even one innocent drug calculated to produce a certain effect, in place of another sent for and designed to produce a different effect. If he does these things he cannot escape civil responsibility upon the alleged pretext that it was an accidental or an innocent mistake. We are asked by the defendants' attorneys in their argument, with some emphasis, if druggists are in legal estimation, to be regarded as insurers. The answer is, we see no good reason why a vendor of drugs, should in his business be entitled to a relaxation of the rule which applies to vendors of provisions, which is, that the vendor undertakes and insures that the article is wholesome (h).

The general customer is not supposed to be skilled in the matter of drugs, but in the purchase he must rely upon the druggist to furnish the article called for; and in this particular business the customer who has not the experience and learning necessary to a proper vending of drugs, will not be held to the rule that he must examine for himself, it would be but idle mockery for the customer to make the examination when it would avail him nothing. On the contrary, the business is such that in the very nature of things, the druggist must be held to warrant that he will deliver the drug called for and purchased by the customer (i).

It is the duty of the druggist to know whether his drugs are sound or not, and it is no answer to his want of knowledge to say, that the buyer had opportunities for inspection, and could judge for himself of the quality of goods (j).

If a druggist miscompounds a medicine, or intentionally deviates from the formula, he commits a tortious act, and

(h) 13 B. Monr. 219.
(i) *Jones* v. *George*, 13 Rep. 738; Tex. Sup. Ct. (1882).
(j) Chitty on Contracts, p. 393.

if any injury arises to another through his ignorance or neglect he is liable.  Even if a physician writes a prescription wrongly it is expected that the druggist will know enough to detect the error, and whether he does so or not he still compounds it at his peril.  For one man's negligence or omission of duty is no palliation of another's, and under the doctrine of joint liability the apothecary or druggist who compounds, knowingly or not, a noxious prescription, commits a joint tort with the physician who writes it (*k*).  And in an action against a druggist for injury through the negligence of his clerk in selling sulphate of zinc for Epsom salts, it is no defence to say that the subsequent medical treatment was negligent (*l*).

A wholesale druggist is liable in the same way as a retail, when he supplies substances notoriously dangerous to health or life, and he impliedly warrants the articles to be as represented by their conventional designation, and if they are not so, he is liable for all damages that may ensue from his misrepresentation (*m*).

If a druggist affixes to a medicine, or drug, a label bearing his name and stating it to have been prepared by him, he makes the warrant only more notorious, and by so doing (inasmuch as it is an invitation to the public to confide in his representation), is ever after estopped from denying responsibility for any injury which may have arisen out of defects in its quality, or errors in its composition.  So long as the label is attached, it is an affirmation of the good quality of the article and its correct composition, to every one who relies upon it when buying.  But as some articles deteriorate in time, what is said in relation to the liability of the vendor applies only to the article at the time it leaves

---

(*k*) *Howe* v. *Young*, 16 Ind. 312 ; 2 Hilliard on Torts, p. 297, sec. A.

(*l*) *Brown* v. *Marshall*, 47 Mich. 576.

(*m*) *VanBracken* v. *Fondar*, 12 John. 468 ; *Jones* v. *Murray*, 3 Monr. 85 ; *Marshall* v. *Peck*, 1 Dana. 609.

his hands. He only warrants its good qualities then, but no longer, and his representation affirms that much, and no more (*n*). The subject of labels was carefully considered in *Thomas* v. *Winchester* (*o*), where Ruggles C.J. gave judgment. Mary Ann Thomas was ordered a dose of extract of dandelion, her husband bought what he believed was dandelion from Dr. Foord, druggist and physician; but it was extract of belladonna. The jar was labelled '½ ℔. dandelion, prepared by A. Gilbert, No. 108 John street, N. Y.' Foord bought it as dandelion from James S. Aspinwall, druggist, who bought it from defendant, a druggist, 108 John street. Defendant manufactured some drugs and purchased others, but labelled all in the same way. Gilbert was an assistant who had originally owned the business. The extract in the jar had been purchased from another dealer. The two extracts are alike in colour, consistency, smell and taste. Gilbert's labels were paid for by defendant and used in his business with his knowledge and consent. A non-suit was moved for on the ground, that defendant being a remote vendor and there being no privity or connection between him and the plaintiff, the action could not be sustained. The Court said, "Gilbert, the defendant's agent, would have been punishable for manslaughter if Mrs. Thomas had died in consequence of taking the falsely labelled medicine. Every one who by his culpable negligence causes the death of another, although without intent to kill, is guilty of manslaughter (*p*). This rule applies not only where the death of one is occasioned by the neglectful act of another, but where it is caused by the neglectful omission of a duty by that other (*q*). Although the defendant W. may not be answerable criminally for the neglect

(*n*) Ordronaux, secs. 183-184.
(*o*) 2 Selden, 397, (N. Y.)
(*p*) 2 R. S. sec. 662, 319.
(*q*) 2 Car. & Kir. 368.

of his agent, there can be no doubt as to his liability in a civil action, in which the action of the agent is to be regarded as the act of the principal. The defendant's neglect put human life in imminent danger. Can it be said that there was no duty on the part of the defendant to avoid the creation of that danger by the exercise of greater caution? Or that the exercise of that caution was a duty only to his immediate vendee, whose life was not endangered? (He being a dealer and not a customer.) The defendant's duty arose out of the nature of his business, and the danger to others incident to its mismanagement. Nothing but mischief like that which actually happened could have been expected from sending the poison falsely labelled into the market, and the defendant is justly responsible for the probable consequences of the act. The duty of exercising caution in this respect did not arise out of the defendant's contract of sale to Aspinwall. The wrong done by the defendant was in putting the poison unlabelled into the hands of Aspinwall as an article of merchandise to be sold, and afterwards used, as the extract of dandelion by some person then unknown. The defendant's contract of sale to Aspinwall does not excuse the wrong done the plaintiffs. It was part of the means by which the wrong was effected. The plaintiffs' injury and their remedy would have stood on the same principle if the defendant had given the belladonna to Dr. Foord without price, or if he had put it in his shop without his knowledge under circumstances that would have led to its sale on the faith of the labels."

Ordronaux says (sec. 186): It cannot be denied that had Mrs. Thomas died, Foord would, equally with Gilbert, have been guilty of manslaughter, since whether he intended it or no, he was doing an unlawful act in dispensing a poison for a salutary medicine. While then it may be proper enough to rely upon labels and warranties of others, in dealing with ordinary substances, still when it comes to articles of a character dangerous to health or life, the law will presume knowledge of their quality in those professionally dealing in them, and exact a degree of skill and care commensurate with the risks incurred. Here it is *caveat venditor* instead of *caveat emptor*.

In Kentucky, a druggist sold croton oil instead of linseed oil for a patient, who, in consequence of the mistake, died. His widow was held entitled to full damages against the seller (*r*).

If a druggist negligently sell a deadly poison as and for a harmless medicine to A., who buys it to administer to B., and gives B. a dose of it as a medicine, from the effect of which he dies, a right of action against the druggist survives to B.'s representative, notwithstanding the want of privity of contract between B. and the druggist (*s*). And this is the rule, also, when the sale has been made by the apothecary's assistant (*t*).

Joseph George, and Emma, his wife, sued Skivington, a druggist, alleging that he, in the course of his business, professed to sell a chemical compound made of ingredients known only to him, and by him represented to be fit for a hairwash without causing injury to the person that used it, and to have been carefully compounded by him; that Joseph thereupon bought of the defendant a bottle of this hairwash, to be used by Emma, as the defendant knew, and on the terms that it could be so safely used, and had been so compounded; yet the defendant had so negligently and unskilfully conducted himself in preparing and selling the hairwash, that it was unfit to be used for washing the hair, whereby the plaintiff, Emma, who used it for that

(*r*) *Hansford* v. *Payne*, 11 Bush. 380.
(*s*) *Norton* v. *Sewall*, 106 Mass. 143.
(*t*) *Ibid.*

purpose was injured. The Court held that a good cause of action was shewn (*u*).

A Massachusetts apothecary sold sulphide of antimony by mistake for black oxide of manganese. The two look alike, but differ in this, that the preparation of manganese may be safely mixed with chlorate of potassia for many useful purposes; but if that antimony is mixed with that chlorate, an explosive compound is formed. The buyer, supposing he had manganese, proceeded to mix it with potassia, having bought the article for that purpose. But, it being antimony, the compound which he made exploded, broke his head, damaged his hearing, and destroyed the furniture of his laboratory. Yet the Court held that the druggist was not chargeable with these damages, because he did not know that the article he sold was to be mixed with potassia, and did not sell it for that purpose. Kept or used by itself, as he sold it, it would have been innocuous. He was not to blame for the mixing, the real cause of the injury (*v*).

In England (*w*), a chemist and druggist was indicted for manslaughter, but was acquitted. The deceased had been in the constant habit of getting aconite and occasionally henbane from Noakes; on this occasion he sent two bottles of his own, one marked, "Henbane, 30 drops at a time." The druggist by mistake put the aconite into the henbane bottle, the dose of thirty drops was taken, and the customer was no more. Erle, C.J., told the jury that although there might be evidence of negligence sufficient for a civil action, still that they could not convict unless there was such a degree of complete negligence as the law meant by the word "felonious," and that in this case he did not think there

(*u*) *George* v. *Skivington*, L. R. 5 Exch. 1.
(*v*) *Davidson* v. *Nicholls*, 11 Allen, 514.
(*w*) *R.* v. *Noakes*, 4 F. & F. 920.

was sufficient to warrant that. But Tessymond, a chemist's apprentice, was found guilty of manslaughter for causing the death of an infant by negligently giving to a customer who asked for paregoric to give to the infant (a child of nine weeks old), a bottle with a paregoric label, but containing laudanum, and recommending a dose of ten drops ($x$).

One Jones recovered against a chemist and druggist of the name of Fay, £100 for damages, because he, Fay, gave him blue pills for the painters' colic, such physic being improper ($y$). A man, on the advice of a friend, went to a drug store for ten cents worth of "black-draught," a comparatively harmless drug, of which he intended to take a small glassful as a dose for diarrhœa. There was evidence given by the clerk who sold the mixture, that at the shop he asked for "black-drops," the defendant, the proprietor, told him that that was poison, that the dose was from ten to twelve drops, and advised him to take another mixture; he refused, and the clerk (by the defendant's direction), gave him two drachms of "black-drops" in a bottle, with a label bearing those two words written upon it, but nothing to indicate the dose, or that it was poison. The man took the bottle home, drank almost all its contents, and died the next morning from the effects of so doing. In an action brought by the representative of the deceased to recover damages for negligent killing by the defendant, it was held that the Courts should have submitted to the jury the question as to whether the defendant was not guilty of negligence in failing to place upon the bottle a label, shewing that its contents were poisonous, and that it erred in non-suiting the plaintiff. Afterwards in giving the judgment of the Court of Appeal, Finch, J., said, "on such a state of facts (as sworn to by the clerk) a verdict

($x$) 1 Lewin C. C. 169.
($y$) 4 F. & F. 525.

against the defendant would not be justified. Although no label marked 'poison' was put upon the phial, and granting that by such omission the defendant was guilty of misdemeanor and liable to the penalty of the criminal law (under the statute of the State), still that fact does not make him answerable to the customer injured, or to his representative in case of his death, for either a negligent or wrongful act, when towards that customer he was guilty of neither, since he fairly and fully warned him of all and more than could have been made known by the authorized label.   \*   \*   \*   If the warning was in truth given, if the deceased was cautioned that the medicine sold was a strong poison, and but ten or twelve drops must be taken, he had all the knowledge and all the warning that the label could have given, and could not disregard it and then charge the consequences of his own negligent reckless act upon the seller of the poison. But if no such warning was given, its omission was negligence, for the results of which the vendor was liable both at common law and by force of the statute." But the Court considered that the clerk being himself the one who had been negligent stood in a position to provoke suspicion, arouse doubt and justify watchful and rigid criticism, and that this joined with the conduct of the deceased, developed a question of fact rather than of law, and that the Court below was right in saying that the case should have been submitted to the jury (z).

Under the Ontario Pharmacy Act no one can sell certain poisons named without having the word "Poison," and the name of the article, distinctly labelled upon the package; and if the sale is by retail, the name of the proprietor of the establishment where it is sold, and the address must also be on the label (a).

(z) *Wohlfarht* v. *Beckert*, 27 Hun, 74 : 92 N.Y. 490.
(a) R. S. O., c. 145, sec. 27.

Any person selling any poison, in violation of the Act, is liable to a penalty of not more than $20 and costs for the first offence, and $50 and costs for every subsequent offence; and one-half of the penalty goes to the prosecutor; and no one selling in violation of the Act can recover his charges. And one wilfully or knowingly selling any article under pretence that it is a particular drug or medicine, when it is not, is liable to the above penalties, besides any other to which he may be liable irrespective of the Act (*b*).

In Georgia it was held, that where a druggist in good faith recommended the prescription of another person to the owner of a sick horse, who thereupon ordered him to put it up and paid for it, the owner had no cause of action because the medicine had injured his horse, as the stuff was properly prepared according to the prescription (*c*).

In England chemists and druggists are liable to the heavy penalty of £500 if they sell to brewers or dealers in beer anything to be used as a substitute for malt; they are also liable for adulterating, or selling any adulterated, medicine; and on a second offence of this kind, the name of the offender, his abode, and his crime may be published in the newspapers at his expense (*d*).

An action can be maintained by a husband against a druggist to recover damages for selling to the plaintiff's wife, secretly, from day to day large quantities of laudanum to be used by her as a beverage, and which are so used by her to the druggist's knowledge, without the knowledge or consent of the husband, the druggist well knowing that the same was injuring and impairing her health, and concealing the fact of such sales and the use thereof from the husband;

---
(*b*) Sections, 28-31.
(*c*) *Ray* v. *Burbank*, 6 Ga. 505.
(*d*) 56 Geo. III. cap. 58, sec. 3; 31 & 32 Vict. cap. 121, sec. 24; 23 & 24 Vict. cap. 84, sec. 30.

in consequence of which use by her the wife became sick and emaciated, and her mind was affected, so that she was unable to perform her duties as such wife, and her affections became alienated from her husband, and he lost her society, and was compelled to expend divers sums of money in medical and other attendance upon her (*e*).

In some of the American Courts it has been held that a statute forbidding the sale or keeping for sale without authority of spirituous or intoxicating liquors does not apply to druggists who keep such liquors only for the purpose of mixing them with other ingredients, according to prescriptions of physicians; and also for the purpose of manufacturing such compounds as are commonly used by druggists to be sold as medicines for remedies for sickness and disease (*f*). The question has often come up whether a compound sold by a druggist is to be considered an intoxicating liquor, the sale of which is illegal, or not. The rule laid down is, that so so long as liquors retain their characters as intoxicating liquors, capable of being used as beverages, notwithstanding that other ingredients—roots or tinctures—may have been mixed therewith, they fall under the ban of the law; but when they are so compounded with other substances as to lose their distinctive characters of intoxicating liquors, and are no longer desirable for use as stimulating beverages, they are medicine and their sale is not prohibited (*g*).

In Indiana a *bona fide* sale of intoxicating liquor by a druggist for medicinal purposes is not a violation of the statute regulating the sale of such liquors, although the statute contains no exception authorizing the sale of such

---

(*e*) *Hoard* v. *Peck*, 56 Barb. 202.

(*f*) *Common.* v. *Ramsdell*, 130 Mass. 68.

(*g*) *State* v. *Laffer*, 38 Iowa, 422; *Common.* v. *Ramsdell*, supra; *Common.* v. *Hallett*, 103 Mass. 452; *Common.* v. *Butterrick*, 6 Cush. 247.

liquors, without license, for medicinal, chemical or sacramental purposes.

And that is the law in North Carolina, but not in Arkansas (*h*). In Iowa it was considered a breach of the law for a druggist to sell a quart of whiskey to a stranger upon his simple statement that he was accustomed to take it as a medicine and wanted it as such (*i*).

In Texas, where a druggist can only sell ardent spirits upon the prescription of physicians in sickness, a druggist who is himself a physician may sell to a sick patient without a prescription from anyone else (*j*).

(*h*) *Nixon* v. *State,* 76 Ind. 524; *State* v. *Wray,* 72 N. C. 253; *Woods* v. *State,* 36 Ark. 36 ; S. c. 38 Am. Rep. 22.

(*i*) *State* v. *Knowles,* 57 Iowa, 669.

(*j*) *Boone* v. *State,* 10 Tex. Ct. App. 418.

## CHAPTER XV.

### PARTNERS, GOODWILL, ASSISTANTS.

A partnership (*a*) between medical men is an association of persons, standing to one another in the relation of principals, for jointly carrying out the objects of their profession, with an agreement to share the profits.

The general laws relating to partnerships apply to those of medical men or dentists. There can be no partnership, as between themselves, if the relationship of master and servant exists, or where there is no joint interest. No particular form of words is needed to create a partnership, nor need the agreement be in writing unless it is to last for more than a year from the date. If an agreement to form a partnership is broken an action will lie, if the terms of the agreement be clear and distinct; but the performance of such an agreement will not be compelled unless all the terms have been fixed and ascertained, and a definite time for its duration agreed on.

If one has been induced to enter the partnership through the fraud or misrepresentation of the other, the party deceived may at his option avoid the contract. But he should act promptly on discovering the deception. Where a surgeon was induced to enter into partnership with, and pay a large premium to another, in consequence of mis-

---

(*a*) See Glenn's Laws, cap. viii.

representations as to the amount of income derived from the practice, a dissolution was decreed and a return of part of the premium (b); and where a practitioner took a partner and a premium, and agreed to continue practising for three years, concealing the fact that he was suffering from a disease which soon carried him off, his executor was ordered to return part of the premium (c).

Partners are trustees and agents for one another, and must exercise the most perfect good faith towards one another. One cannot sue the other for his share of the profits until the accounts have been stated and settled between them. One medical man cannot, as a rule, bind his partner by borrowing money, even to pay partnership liabilities, or by making or drawing promissory notes or bills of exchange; but he may generally do so by simple contracts, within the scope of the business.

In England, it appears that there is nothing illegal in the partnership of a qualified and an unqualified practitioner, and that it will be sufficient if only one member of the firm be registered (d).

A partnership may be dissolved by mutual agreement, or by the effluxion of time. A wilful and permanent neglect of business is a ground for dissolution; so is gross misconduct by a partner in reference to partnership matters. Immoral conduct materially affecting the business will be a ground for dissolution; also, insanity, or permanent incapacity (e). On a dissolution the partners may separately carry on the business at any place, unless restrained by agreement.

(b) *Jauncey* v. *Knowles*, 29 L. J. Cha. 95.
(c) *Mackenna* v. *Parkes*, 36 L. J. Cha. 366.
(d) *Turner* v. *Reynall*, 14 C. B. N. S. 328. See, also, *Reg.* v. *Tefft*, 45 Ont. Q. B. 144.
(e) *Anon.*, cited 2 K. & J. 446.

Sir John Leach considered that in a partnership, between professional persons, upon the death of one partner the good-will of the business belonged to the survivor, and that he was not bound to account to the representatives of the deceased partner for it (*f*).

A good-will attaches to a professional, as well as to any other kind of business, and it is and may be the subject of purchase and sale ; and although it is not computable, and the sale of it is not enforceable by an action for specific performance if it has not been estimated, yet it does stand on the same footing as any other business, if the parties have fixed a determinate price upon it, or have provided any other way of fixing its value (*g*). The good-will of a medical man's business is an asset of his estate which his representatives can sell, and for which they must account if it is sold. But it is not clear that the representatives can be compelled to find a purchaser (*h*).

Jessel, M. R., recently asked the question, "What is the meaning of selling a medical practice?" And in answering his query he said, "It is the selling of the introduction of the patients of the doctor who sells to the doctor who buys, he has nothing else to sell except the introduction. He can persuade his patients, probably, who have confidence in him to employ the gentleman he introduces as being a qualified man, and fit to undertake the cure of their maladies, but that is all he can do. Therefore, when you talk of the sale of a non-dispensing medical practice—of course, when a man keeps what is called a doctor's shop, there is a different thing entirely to sell—you are really talking of the sale of the introduction to the patients, and the length, the

---

(*f*) *Farr* v. *Pearce*, 3 Mad. 74 ; *Austen* v. *Boys*, 24 Beav. 598 ; 2 DeG. & J. 626.

(*g*) *McIntyre* v. *Belcher*, 10 Jur. N. S. 239.

(*h*) *Christie* v. *Clark*, 16 (Ont.) C. P. 544 ; 27 Q. B. 21.

character and duration of the introduction, the terms of the introduction are everything. And there is something more, according to my experience, in cases of the sale of medical practices; there is always a stipulation that the selling doctor shall retire from practice either altogether or within a given distance. It is so always, and there is also sometimes a stipulation that he will not solicit the patients, or shall not solicit them for a given time. They are both very important stipulations as regards keeping together the practice for the purchasing doctor " (*i*).

The general rule of law is, that any contract in general restraint of trade or industry is illegal and void as contrary to public policy; but such contracts are valid if they operate merely as a partial restraint, and are made for good consideration, and not unreasonable. Whether they are reasonable or not, is for the Court, not the jury, to say. A contract made with an assistant, or with a partner, that upon separating from the principal, or partner, he will not practise within a certain section of country, or for a certain time, is valid when made in consideration of instruction to be given, or pecuniary or other benefits to be enjoyed in consequence of the partnership. The limits must be reasonable, and when the contract is not to practise within so many miles of a certain place, the distance will be measured "as the crow flies," unless otherwise mentioned (*j*).

Covenants, on the part of an assistant to a surgeon and apothecary, not to practise on his own account for fourteen years, in a certain town, or within ten miles of the town; and not at any time to practise within five, seven, ten, twenty miles of certain places, have been all respectively

(*i*) *May* v. *Thomson*, L. R. 20 Ch. D. 718.
(*j*) *Dingnan* v. *Walker*, 33 L. T. 256.

held good (*k*). The comparative populousness of the district forbidden ought not to enter into consideration at all; and an assistant to a dentist was held bound by a covenant not to practise in London, notwithstanding that city had a population of over a million (*l*). But a stipulation not to practise within one hundred miles of York, in consideration of receiving instruction in dentistry, was held void (*m*).

A promise, whether verbal or written, made without good consideration by a medical man not to exercise or carry on his profession within certain limits is void. The stipulations in a contract not to practise are divisible, and if part of them be unreasonable, and therefore illegal and void, the agreement is not void altogether; and the remaining stipulations, if valid, will not be affected by the illegality of the others (*n*).

The relations of medical men to their apprentices, assistants and pupils, are, as a rule, regulated by the ordinary law of master and servant. No particular words are needed to create the relationship of master and apprentice, or master and assistant, the intention of the parties will be considered, nor need the agreement be in writing, unless it is not to be performed within a year from the making thereof (*o*). A master is liable on contracts entered into by his apprentice or assistant, when he has authorized him to enter into any such contract, either expressly, or by implication. For instance, if an assistant usually orders drugs

---

(*k*) *Davis* v. *Mason*, 5 T. R. 118; *Carnes* v. *Nesbitt*, 7 H. & N. 778; *Sainter* v. *Ferguson* 7 C. B. 716; *Hastings* v. *Whitley*, 2 Ex. 611; *Haynard* v. *Young*, 2 Chit. 407; *McClurg's Appeal*, 58 P. St. 51; Parsons on Contracts, vol. ii. p. 748.

(*l*) *Mallan* v. *May*, 11 M. & W. 653.

(*m*) *Horner* v. *Graves*, 7 Bing. 735.

(*n*) *Mallan* v. *May*, supra. Generally on this subject, see Glenn's Laws, cap. viii.

(*o*) Glenn's Laws, cap. viii.

on credit, and the master usually pays, the master will be held liable to pay for any goods of a similar nature which the assistant may get for his own and not his master's use (*p*). The master is also, as a rule, liable to a civil action for the wrongful acts of his assistant, unless they be beyond the ordinary scope of his employment; the plaintiff, however, must prove that the injury was produced by want of proper skill, where the act complained of is said to have arisen through want of skill (*q*). But the master will not be criminally responsible for the acts of his assistant or apprentice, if the latter has caused the death of any one, unless, indeed, he has expressly commanded or taken part in the acts (*r*). In a case of criminal negligence, the apprentice himself is responsible; if a party is guilty of negligence, and death results, the party guilty of that negligence is also guilty of manslaughter.

An apprentice, or pupil, cannot be dismissed in as summary a way as an ordinary servant for misconduct. In one case it was held that though a person has a right to dismiss a servant for misconduct, still he has no right to turn away an apprentice because he misbehaves; and that the case of a young man, say of seventeen, who under a written agreement, is placed with a medical man as "pupil and assistant," and with whom a premium is paid, is a case between that of apprenticeship and service; and if such an one on some occasions comes home intoxicated, this alone will not justify the surgeon in dismissing him. But if the "pupil and assistant," by employing the shop boy to compound the medicines, occasions real danger to the surgeon's practice, this would justify the surgeon in dismissing him (*s*).

(*p*) *Nickson* v. *Brohan*, 10 Mod. 109.
(*q*) *Hancke* v. *Hooper*, 7 C. & P. 81.
(*r*) *R.* v. *Bennett*, 29 L. J.; M. C. 27; *R.* v. *Tessymond*, 1 Lewin C. C. 169.
(*s*) *Wise* v. *Wilson*, 1 C. & K. 662.

Pupils and others admitted to hear the lectures of medical men, whether such lectures are delivered *ex-tempore*, or from memory, or from notes, although they may go to the extent, if they are able to do so, of taking down the whole by means of shorthand, can do so only for the purposes of their own information, and cannot publish the lectures for profit without the consent of the lecturer (*t*).

(*t*) *Abernethy* v. *Hutchinson*, 3 L. J. 209; *Nicols* v. *Pitman*, L. R. 26 Ch. D. 374.

# INDEX.

## A.

ABORTION—
>Evidence of experts in cases of, 116.
>Criminality of, 146, 147.

ACCIDENT—
>Payment of medical men in cases of, 40, 41.

ACCOUNT—
>Must be in detail, 22.

ADVERTISING QUACKS—132, 133.

AMPUTATED LIMBS—
>Ownership of, 143.

ANATOMY—
>A lawful study, 154, 157, 158.
>Hindrances to study of, 149, 152.
>In early days, 149, 150.
>Provision made for study of, in England, 150, 153.
>" " in Canada, 151, 156.
>" " in United States, 155, 156.

ANATOMY ACT OF 1832—153.

ANGUINEUM—2.

APOTHECARIES—
>In England in early days, 11.
>Incorporated in England, 12.
>How regulated, 12.
>Duties of, 12.
>Fees of, 15, 16.

ARTIFICIAL TEETH.—*See* TEETH.

ASSAULTS ON PATIENTS—
    Attempting carnal intercourse with, 144.
    Wantonly stripping patient, 144.
    Taking layman to midwifery case, 144.
    Liability for committing one as insane, 146.

ASSISTANTS AND APPRENTICES—
    Rules regulating, 193.
    Master liable for, civilly, 193, 194.
        "    not liable criminally, 194.
        "    may recover for services of, 20.
    Misconduct of, 194.

ATTENDANCE—
    Medical men neglecting, 72, 73.
    Withdrawing from, 73, 74.

## B.

BARBERS—
    As practitioners, 4, 5, 6.

BAUNSCHEIDT SYSTEM—
    Layman practising, 47.
    Liability for using, 89.

BODIES—
    Supply of, for dissecting, 150-156.

BODY-SNATCHING—*See* RESURRECTION, 152-157.

BOOKS—*See* SCIENTIFIC BOOKS, 99-105.

BOTANIC PHYSICIANS—52, 54, 88.

## C.

CARELESSNESS—*See* NEGLIGENCE.
    Of patient, 67-69.
    When physician criminally liable for, 85-88, 91.
    In treating internal diseases, 92.

CHARACTER—
    Defamation of, when actionable, 131, 134.

CHEMIST AND DRUGGIST—*See* DRUGGISTS.

CHLOROFORM—
 Care needed in using, 163-166.

CIVIL LIABILITY—
 For negligence—*See* NEGLIGENCE.
 For stealing corpse, 157.

CLAIRVOYANT PHYSICIAN—
 Must be licensed in Maine, 52.
 Misrepresentations by, 142.

CLERICAL PRACTITIONERS—3.

COMMUNICATIONS BETWEEN PHYSICIAN AND PATIENT—
 When not privileged, 93.
 When privileged, 94-96.

CONSULTATIONS—23.

CONTAGIOUS DISEASES—
 Precautions necessary when attending, 21, 143.
 Exposing people suffering from, 147.

CONTRIBUTORY NEGLIGENCE—
 Of patient, 67-69.

CORPSE—
 Stealing, 152.
 Who owns the, 153.
 Selling, 153.
 Raising, a misdemeanor, 154-156.
 Civil liability for raising, 157.
 Exhuming, when ordered, 159.

CRIMINAL LIABILITY—*See* CRIMINAL|MALPRACTICE.

CRIMINAL MALPRACTICE—
 Definition of, 55, 82.
 Felonious intent in, 82.
 Immaterial whether physician licensed or not, 83, 84, 91.
 What makes, 84, 85.
 Physician acting honestly and *bonâ fide*, 89, 92.
 Mistakes of druggists, 180, 181.

CRITICISM—
    When justifiable, 132, 133.

CURE—
    Not essential to right to pay, 20, 21.
    No cure, no pay, 24.
    Promising, 143.
    Curious cures, 2, 3, 8.

CONTRACT—
    Between physician and patient, 141.
    Not to practice, 192, 193.

## D.

DAMAGES—
    For personal injuries, 78, 80.
    Rules for determining, 78, 79.
    Not recoverable against representatives, 80.
    In cases of death, 80, 81.
    Only one action for same cause, 81.
    Against negligent druggists, 177-185.
        "         "      dentists, 162-167.

DEATH—
    Damages when negligence causes, 80, 81.
    Evidence of experts as to cause of, 116-119.

DECLARATIONS OF SICK PEOPLE—
    When evidence, 96-98.

DEFAMATION—129-137.
    What libel, what slander, 129.
    When actionable, 129, *et seq*.
    Civil and criminal remedies, 130.
    Imputing want of knowledge, 130.
        "     unprofessional conduct, 131-132.
        "     immorality, 134.
    Holding up to ridicule, 132.
    Justifiable criticism not, 132, 133.
    Evidence in actions for, 135.
    When physician liable for, 135-137.

DENTISTS—Chapter XIII.
>Early practitioners, 160, 161.
>Subjects of examination for, 161, 162.
>In Ontario, must be licensed, 162.
>Liability for negligence, 162, 167.
>Pulling wrong tooth, 163, 167.
>Skill requirable, 164, 166.
>Acting gratuitously, 166.
>When services are useless, 167.
>Are they mechanics? 169, 170.
>Defrauding patient, 171, 172.
>Appropriating signs of others, 172.

DILIGENCE—
>Must go along with skill, 64.

DIPLOMA—
>*Prima facie* proof of skill, 64.

DISCRETION—
>As to modes of treatment, 25.
>As to number of visits, 63.

DISSECTION—
>Provisions made for, 150, 151.
>English Anatomy Act, 153.
>Lawfulness of, considered, 157, 158.

DRUGGISTS—Chapter XIV.
>Definition, 174.
>Old time, 175.
>Requirements of, 175-176.
>Liability for miscompounding, 176-178.
>" " mistakes, 177-185.
>" " quality of drug, 178.
>" criminally, 180.
>" for selling adulterating substances, 186.
>" " " deleterious drugs, 186.
>" " " intoxicants, 187, 188.
>Warrants drug to be as represented, 179.
>Label a warranty, 179-180.

DRUGS—
>Physician may charge for, 24.
>Mistakes in selling, 177-186.

DRUIDS—1-3.

DUEL—
    Medical man attending, 144.

DUTY OF PHYSICIAN—
    On undertaking charge of patient, 57.
    Not bound to take charge, 57.
    To possess ordinary care, diligence and knowledge, 58-61.
    In cases of small-pox, 22, 144, 147.

DYING DECLARATIONS—
    Evidence in certain cases, 105.

## E.

EARLY PRACTITIONERS—Chapter I.

ENGLAND—
    Early practitioners in—Chapter I.
    Who may practice, 43.
    Women may practice, 14.

ENTRIES AGAINST INTEREST—
    Admissible as evidence, 105, 106.

EXPERIMENTS—
    Liability on making, 71, 72, 168.

EVIDENCE—*See* EXPERTS AND EXPERT EVIDENCE, SCIENTIFIC BOOKS.

EXPERTS AND EXPERT EVIDENCE—
    Fees to medical witnesses, 27, *et seq*,
    Excluding at trial, 106, 120.
    Limiting number at trial, 106.
    Rules for guidance, 106, 107.
    When evidence of, admitted, 108, 117-120, 127.
    Who may be experts, 109-114, 128.
    The Court decides who may be, 113, 114.
    Experts among the Romans, 109.
    Opinions concerning, 110, 121-124.
    Need not have made a special study, 112.
    Better if they have, 112, 127.
    Jury to decide weight to be given to, 114.
    Opinions on morals, 115.

EXPERTS AND EXPERT EVIDENCE—*Continued.*
>Do not speak as to merits, 115, 118, 125, 127.
>Advisers of the Court, 115, 116.
>Should state grounds of opinion, 116.
>Admissible only as to matters of skill, 119.
>Are not jurors, 119, 125.
>Opinions on opinion, 119.
>In insanity cases, 121-128.
>What they may be asked, 124, 125.
>Must hear all the evidence, 126.
>Hypothetical cases, how put, 126, 127.

## F.

FAMILY PHYSICIAN—
>Recommending another, 148.

FEES—*See* PAYMENT OF MEDICAL MEN.
>Under Roman Law, 15.
>Of physicians, not recoverable at Common Law, 15, 16.
>Recoverable under Medical Act, 15, 17.
>Of surgeons and apothecaries, 15, 16.
>Of physician and surgeon, 16.
>In Scotland and the Colonies, 17.
>In America, 17.
>No express promise to pay necessary, 18.
>How fixed, 18, 19.
>Must be reasonable, 19.
>In some countries fixed by law, 19.
>Services of assistants, 20.
>Not dependant upon cure, 20, 21.
>But services must be of benefit, 20-24, 167.
>Account should be in detail, 23.
>For friendly visits, 24.
>For drugs, 24.
>Where no cure, no pay, 25.
>To medical witnesses, 26, 27.
>To medical experts, 27-31.
>Exorbitant charges, 140.
>Who must pay, 32.

FRANCE—
>Who may practise in, 44.

FRIEND—
    Prescribing as, fees, 24.
    Not medical attendant, 24.

## G.

GERMANY—
    Who may practise in, 44.

GIFTS TO MEDICAL MEN—
    Are closely watched, 139.
    When set aside, 139, 140.
    When sustained, 140, 141.

GOODWILL—
    In professional partnerships, 191.
    Sale of, 191.

GRATUITOUS SERVICES—
    Liability of physicians for, 61, 65, 66.
        "    " unprofessional men, 66, 67.
        "    " dentists, 166.

GROSS NEGLIGENCE—
    What is, 87, 88.
    Liability for, 55.

## H

HAIR-DYE—
    Noxious, damages for, 182.

HOMŒOPATHISTS—
    Regulations as to, in Ontario, 66.
    Are Physicians in New York, 50, 54.
    Are not Quacks, 132.
    Consulting with, 134.

HUSBAND—
    When liable for attendance on wife, 35, 39.
    When liable for artificial teeth for wife, 171.
    Suing druggist for damages to wife's health, 186.

HYPOTHETICAL CASE—
    How put, 126, 127.

# I

IGNORANCE—

    Liability for gross ignorance, 55-61.
    Criminal liability for gross, 55-88, 91, 92.
    Imputing, when actionable, 130.

IMMORALITY—

    When actionable to impute, 134.

IMPROPER TREATMENT—

    When a defence to action, 20-24, 167.
    Charges for, 20, 22, 167.

INFANT—

    Medicines and medical aid, necessary for, 39.

INFECTIOUS DISORDERS—

    Exposing persons suffering from, 147.
    Duty of physicians in cases of, 22, 143, 147.

INSANE PATIENT—

    Not liable for negligence, 69.

INSANITY CASES—

    Evidence of experts, 121-128.
    Opinions concerning, experts in, 121-124.
    When expert evidence admissible, 124.
    How to examine witnesses, 124-125.
    Putting hypothetical cases, 126, 127.
    Evidence of non-experts, 128.
    Experts can only give opinions, 129.
    Liability for committing in, 145-146.
    Requisites for committal, 146.

INTOXICATING LIQUORS—

    When unlawful to give, 148.
    Druggists selling, 187-188.

IRELAND—

    Early practitioners in, 6.

## L

LABEL OF DRUGGIST—
>Is a warranty, 179-180.

LECTURES—
>Cannot be published by students attending them, 195.

LIBEL—*See* DEFAMATION.

## M

MALPRACTICE—*See* CRIMINAL MALPRACTICE.
>Defined, 55.
>Consequences of, 55.
>Civil and criminal, 55, 56, 83.
>Some injury must be proved, 76.
>Is a question for the jury, 76.
>Cases of, should be construed in favor of physician, 76, 77.
>Cases against physician rare, 77.
>Actionable to charge one with, 133.

MANIPULATION—
>Practising, without license, 51.

MANSLAUGHTER—*See* CRIMINAL MALPRACTICE.
>Physicians acting honestly and *bona fide*, 89, 90.
>Druggist making mistake, 180-184.

MASTER AND SERVANT—*See* ASSISTANTS AND APPRENTICES.
>Payment of medical attendance, 40.

MEDICAL ACT OF ENGLAND—
>Recovery of fees under, 17.

MEDICAL ACT OF ONTARIO—
>Recovery of fees under, 17.

MEDICAL MAN—
>Chaucer's definition of, 7.
>Had to be graduates in old times, 7.
>Divisions under Henry VIII, 8.
>Qualifications necessary to practise, 9, 48.
>Qualifications under Henry VIII, 10.
>No branches in America or Colonies, 17.

MEDICAL MAN—*Continued*.

    Discretion as to mode of treatment, 25.
    As witnesses, 26.
    Who must pay, 32-41.
    Who may practise, 42.
    The law favors no school, 42, 47.
    Must practise according to school, 52, 53, 54.
    One practising liable as, 54.
    Duties when assuming charge, 57, 72, 73.
    Must exercise ordinary care and diligence, 58.
    Must keep up with the age, 61, 71.
    Not liable for bad nursing, 70.
    Rashly trying new experiments, 71.
    Accepting retainer must attend, 72, 73.
    Withdrawing from attendance, 73, 74.
    Liability when not employed by patient, 74.
    Action against, for defamation, 135-137.
    Administering intoxicants, 148
    Relations with patients, 138-146.
    Care necessary in choosing, 148.

MEDICINE—

    When first studied in England, 6.
    First statute concerning, 8.
    Evidence of experts as to, 118.

MEMORANDA—

    When may be used in court, 98.

MIDWIFE—

    Defamatory words when actionable, 130.

MISREPRESENTATIONS—

    To obtain money, 142, 143.

MISTLETOE—1

MORALS—

    Expert opinions on, 115.

## N.

NECESSARIES—

    Medicine and medical aid, 35, 39.
    Artificial teeth, 171.

NEGLIGENCE OF MEDICAL MEN—

    Communicating contagious diseases, 22.
    Liability for gross negligence, 55.
    Judged from legal stand point, 56.
    Defined, 56, 57.
    Liability for, when causing injury, 57, 63, 167.
    Medical men must exercise reasonable care and diligence, 58.
    Sex no excuse, 61.
    Where services are gratuitous, 65.
        "      "      " voluntary, 65, 66.
    Proximate cause, 69.
    When requested to perform operation, 69.
    Aggravated by nursing, 70.
    General reputation unavailing, 71, 86.
    Injurious treatment, 72.
    Neglecting to attend, 72, 73.
    Where not employed by patient, 74, 75.
    Not liable for every mistake, 75.
    Is a question for the jury, 76.
    Amount of damages recoverable, 78-80.
    Action for, does not survive against representatives, 80.
    Where death is caused by, 80, 81.
    Criminal negligence, 82-85.
    Immaterial whether physician licensed or not, 83, 84.
    Acting *bona fide* no criminal liability, 89, 90.
    Patient affected by mortal disease, 90, 91.
    Imputing want of skill, when actionable, 130, 133.
    Of dentists, 162, *et seq.*
    Of druggists, 177, *et seq.*

NEGLIGENCE OF PATIENT—

    Responsible for careless choice of physician, 53.
    Knowledge of physician's ignorance, 57, 67.
    Disobeying or neglecting orders, 67, 68.
    What is contributory negligence, 68.
    Insane patient's negligence, 69.

NEW YORK—

    Who may practise in, 49-51.

NURSING—

    Aggravating the case, 70.
    Liability of medical man for, 70.

## O.

ONTARIO—
>Who may practise medicine in, 45,
>" dentistry in, 162.
>" as druggists in, 176.

OPINION—*See* EXPERT EVIDENCE.

## P.

PARENT AND CHILD—
>Liablility of parent for doctor's bill, 33.
>Rule in England and United States, 37, 38.
>Statutory liability in England, 38, 39.

PARTNERSHIP AMONG MEDICAL MEN—
>Definition of, 189.
>General rules applicable, 189.
>Fraudulently inducing one to enter into, 189.
>Conduct of partners, 190.
>Dissolution, 190.
>Interest of survivor, 191.

PATIENT—*See* RELATIONS WITH.
>Calling homœopath, 54.
>Physician not bound to take, 57, 72.
>Must exercise prudence in selecting doctor, 67.
>Must co-operate with doctor, 67, 68.
>Must exercise ordinary care and prudence, 68, 69.
>Physician withdrawing from, 73, 74.
>Not employing physician, 74, 75.
>Suffering from mortal disease, 90, 91.
>Submitting to dangerous operation, 91.
>Communication with physician not privileged, 93.

PAYMENT OF MEDICAL MEN—*See* FEES.
>Physician called in by stranger, 32-35.
>Wife may bind husband for, 35, 36.
>As between parent and child, 35-39.
>" master and servant, 40.
>Paupers, 40.
>Liability of railways in accidents, 40, 41.

PECULIAR PEOPLE—38, 39.

PERSIA—
    Medical fees in, 19.

PHARMACY, COLLEGE OF—
    In Ontario, 175, 176.

POISONS—
    Should be marked, 184.
    Selling illegally, 185.

POST MORTEM—
    Fees for, 27.

PRACTISE—
    Who may, 42, *et seq*.
    Contracts not to, 192, 193.

PRACTICE—
    Sale of, 191, 192.

PRIVILEGED COMMUNICATIONS—
    Communications between physician and patient not, 93.
    Are by statute in some States, 94, 95.
    Must be lawful to be, 95.
    Necessary for physician to prescribe, 95.
    Report of officer of insurance company, 96.
    Defamatory statements when, 136, 137.

PROFESSIONAL EVIDENCE—
    Representation by patient as to malady, 96-98.
    Mem. made by physician, 98, 105.
    Scientific books not admissible, 99-105.
    Dying declarations when admissible, 105.
    Entries against interest admissible, 105.
    Rules for guidance of medical witness, 106, 107.
    Exclusion of experts, 120.

## Q.

QUACKS—
    When medical men may be called, 133, 134.
    When not, 132.

## R.

**Rashness**—86.

**Registration of Medical Men**—
>Before recovery of fees, 17, 18, 45.
>Before practice in England and Ontario, 44, 45.
>Who may be registered in England, 44.
>"         "         Ontario, 45.
>Non-registered practitioners are quacks, 133.
>Striking off registry for felony, 148.

**Regular Physician**—
>An allopathic, 51.

**Representation by Patient**—
>As to malady, when evidence, 96-98.

**Reputation**—
>Unavailing in accidents for negligence, 71, 86.

**Restraint of Trade**—
>When such contracts are allowable, 192, 193.

**Resurrection**—
>Stealing winding sheet, 152.
>Taking body a misdemeanor, 154.
>Assisting at, 156.
>Civil liability for, 157.
>Ordered in proper cases, 159.

**Relations with Patients**—
>No one can take advantage of a trust reposed, 138.
>Practitioner must shew fairness of dealings with patients, 138.
>Undue influence, when inferred, 138-140.
>Gifts to medical men set aside, 139, 140.
>Exorbitant charges relieved against, 140.
>When patient has independent advice, 140, 141.
>Contracts open and fair, 141.
>Wills in favour of medical men, 141, 142.
>Misrepresentations by medical men, 142.
>Promises of cure, 143.
>Duties in cases of small-pox, 143.
>Right to limbs, 143.
>Assaults on patients, 144-146.

ROYAL COLLEGE OF PHYSICIANS. Edinburgh—11.

ROYAL COLLEGE OF PHYSICIANS. Ireland—11.

ROYAL COLLEGE OF PHYSICIANS. London—9.

## S.

SALE OF PRACTISE—191, 192.

SCHOOLS OF MEDICINE—
    The law favors no school, 42, 43, 47, 51, 115.
    Physician must practise according to his school 52.
    Considered in determining skill needed, 63, 64.
    Experts may be of any school, 115.

SCIENTIFIC BOOKS—
    Not admissible as evidence, 99.
    Rule different in Iowa and Wisconsin, 100.
    Cannot be read to jury, 100-103.
    Can be used to test witness, 101.
    Can be read to jury in some States, 103-105.
    When cannot be quoted to jury, 105.
    Can be read to the court, 105.

SCOTLAND—
    Early practitioners in, 5.

SIGN—
    An evidence of professional character, 64.
    Of dentists in old days, 161.
    Misleading, 173.

SKILL—
    Physician must have ordinary, 57, 58.
    What is ordinary, or reasonable skill, 59.
    Amount required, 59-62.
        "        " varies, 60, 61.
    Liability if skill not applied, 62.
    Skill and diligence must be joined, 63.
    School considered in determining, 64.
    Proof of skill, 64.
    Required in non-professional, 64, 65.
        "    " volunteer, 65.
        "    " gratuitous services, 65, 66.
        "    " dentists, 162.

SLANDER—*See* DEFAMATION.

SMALL-POX—
    Duties of physician in cases of, 143.
    Innoculation, 147.
    Exposing patients with, 147.

SMITHS—
    As practitioners. 4.

SUPERSTITIOUS PRACTICES—2, 3, 8.

SURGEONS—
    United with barbers, 4-6.
    Union dissolved, 5.
    Qualification under Henry VIII, 9.
    Fees, 15.
    Right to amputated limbs, 143.
    Attending duels, 144.

## T.

TEETH—
    Value of, 166.
    Dentists pulling wrong tooth, 163.
    Artificial, need not be perfect, 163, 168.
    Contract for purchase of, 169.
    Artificial are necessaries, 171.

## U.

UNDUE INFLUENCE—
    When exercised over patient, 138, 140.
    Setting aside will for, 141, 142.
    Exercised by dentist, 171.

UNITED STATES—
    As a rule any one may practise, 47.
    The law sometimes interferes, 47.
    Statutory requirements, 48, 51.

UNPROFESSIONAL MEN—
    Liable for gross negligence, 65.
    Liability for gratuitous services, 66, 67.
    When criminally liable, 92.
    Admitting, at a confinement, 144.

UNREGISTERED PHYSICIAN—
> Practising for reward, 45, 46.
> " " charity, 46.

## V.

VACCINATION—
> Negligence of physician, 22.

VISITS—
> Physician best judge of number, 23.
> As a friend, 24.

VOLUNTEER—
> Held more strictly than one called in, 65, 66.

## W.

WIFE—
> May generally bind husband to pay doctor, 35, 36.
> But husband may select physician, 36.
> Cannot bind him for clairvoyant services, 36.
> Selling deleterious drugs to, 186.

WILL—
> In favour of medical man, 141, 142.

WITNESS—*See* EXPERTS.
> Fees to medical men, 26, 37.

WOMEN PHYSICIANS—
> Among the Druids, 2.
> In England in early times, 2, 3, 10, 14.
> Penalty for practising, 7.
> In Greece and foreign lands, 13.
> In United States, 14.
> In England under the Medical Act, 14.
> In Ontario, 14.
> As liable for negligence as men, 61.

www.ingramcontent.com/pod-product-compliance
Lightning Source LLC
Chambersburg PA
CBHW021837230426
43669CB00008B/998